RAÚL BARRÀGAN SANZ & JEAN-SÉBASTIEN MOISY

VINTAGE ICONS OF FASHION

FROM THE CHANEL 2.55 TO THE ROLEX OYSTER

MITCHELL BEAZLEY

CONTENTS

SHOES

WATCHES

JEWELLERY

ART OF LIVING

WHAT IS VINTAGE?

When discussing or writing about vintage style, it is important to define its scope and limitations so that we can accurately identify its essence. A notable characteristic of the word 'vintage' is that it has no precise definition because, ultimately, we each have our own vision of what vintage means. It is, therefore, essential to agree on its meaning so that we are all reading from the same page. The word has its origins in the world of winemaking; 'vintage' comes from the Old French word for 'wine harvest', *vendange*, and designates the year a wine was made, and, by extension, the years of the best wines. After crossing seas and oceans, the word was adopted by the English language to signify objects that were old but admired. It was therefore quite natural for the world of fashion to quickly embrace its use. It does not refer to any specific era and has no start or end date. For this book, we have decided to apply the term 'vintage' to any object created before 2004. Designs produced after that date are considered modern or even contemporary.

Our selection brings together pieces that have earned a place in the pantheon of fashion icons. For the most part, these are objects that have made a fashion house famous or helped to establish a powerful identity passed down over generations.

At this point, we need to draw a distinction regarding 'It bags'. First appearing in the late 1990s, these creations cannot be considered timeless: they were must-have bags for a season and then disappeared from collections or, in some cases, were reissued years later. Once out of fashion, the popularity of these models and interest in them is almost non-existent, so if you have a good nose for such things, it can be the moment to get a 'good deal'. That said, how do we know whether or when a piece will come back into fashion?

In this book, we combine our two visions, as seen through the eyes of a boutique owner and a fashion expert. Thanks to these jobs, we are always aware of what our customers are looking for, and our selections are based on a shared analysis of the luxury vintage world. We have been guided by pieces that have seen no dip in their popularity since they were first created. On the contrary, these are items that continue to rise in value each year on the resale market. The same can also be said for the modernized versions of models that are regularly reissued by luxury fashion houses.

We invite you to lose yourself in these pages as we pay homage to pieces that will be forever known for their timeless appeal.

Raúl Barràgan Sanz and Jean-Sébastien Moisy

HERMÈS

THE REIGN OF LEATHER GOODS

The history of Hermès began in 1837, when Thierry Hermès opened a harness workshop in Paris. The craftsman quickly established a reputation thanks to the quality of his know-how. In 1880, his son, Charles-Émile Hermès, moved the business to 24 rue du Faubourg Saint-Honoré, where there was enough space to create bespoke saddles and harnesses. It was not until the 1920s that the company began to innovate with new lines when Émile Hermès introduced small leather goods into its collections, followed by textiles, watches, jewellery and shoes.

RECOGNIZING AN HERMÈS: THE LETTER

Since 1971, the fashion house has systematically marked its bags with a letter, which originally appeared in a circle and later a square. Today, the letter has no shape around it. This mark is known as the 'date code' and identifies the year the model was made.

HERMÈS AND NECKTIES

In 1949, Hermès marketed its first tie. The reason for this offering has an amusing backstory: in Cannes, gentlemen without a tie were refused entry to the casino, and these potential customers visited the neighbouring Hermès store to buy one. Spotting an opportunity, the fashion house decided to launch production of the accessory.

THE ZIP FASTENER BY HERMÈS

One of the reasons for the success of Hermès is thanks to a simple system, the zip fastener, which the company decided to perfect and transpose on to leather goods. The fastener was known as a *Fermeture Éclair* in French, with the name registered as a trademark in 1913 (hence the capital letters) and with Hermès retaining exclusive rights to its use at the time. *Éclair* eventually became a common noun and entered the French language to designate any type of zip. This is why old Hermès models feature the word 'Éclair' on the zip pull.

LEATHERS AND FABRICS

RECOGNIZING AN HERMÈS: LEATHERS

The signature leather of Hermès is box calf, a smooth but stiff calfskin that is prone to scratching. In addition to exotic leathers, the fashion house was quick to introduce new leathers such as Courchevel calfskin, which has a particularly hard-wearing grain, followed by Fjord calfskin and Ardennes leather.

Hermès mostly uses grained calfskin, which offers the best possible resilience; lambskin is rarely used because of its fragility. A key concept for the brand is transmission: designs should stand the test of time so that they can be passed down from generation to generation. Each leather has its own specific characteristics and aficionados, meaning that demand for the same model of bag will differ depending on the material used. For example, a 25cm Kelly Sellier in the Epsom calfskin finish is more sought after than in the Chèvre Mysore goatskin, as the former is more familiar to buyers due to its exposure on social media.

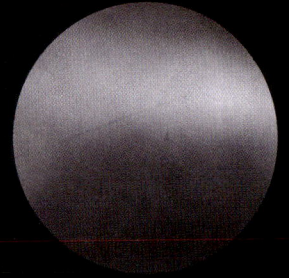

Box calfskin

Courchevel calfskin

Epsom calfskin

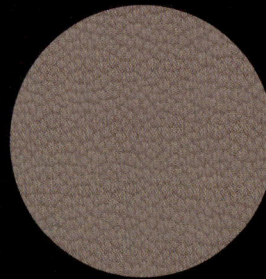

Togo calfskin

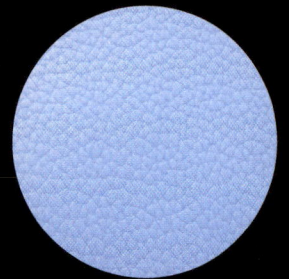

Clemence calfskin

Chèvre Mysore goatskin

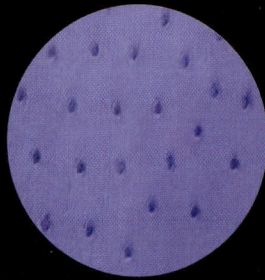

Ostrich skin

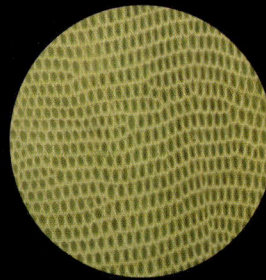

Lizard skin

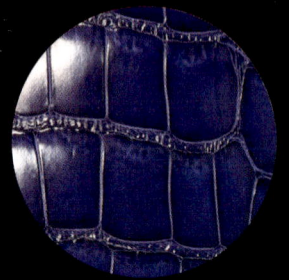

Alligator skin
Alligator mississippiensis

Porosus crocodile skin
Crocodylus porosus

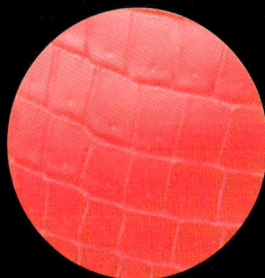

Niloticus crocodile skin
Crocodylus niloticus

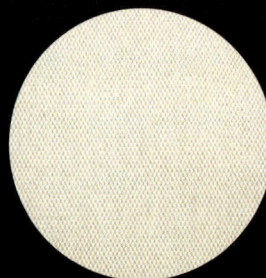

Toile H canvas

Toile chevron canvas

STAMPS

Since the mid-1980s, exotic leathers have been marked with a special stamp to identify the species used to create the bag. This is partly because these pieces are subject to the CITES regulation (Convention on International Trade in Endangered Species), also known as the Washington Convention, an intergovernmental agreement signed in 1973 and ratified by France in 1978. This ensures that protected or endangered species are not overexploited. International trade in certain species is therefore limited and has resulted in some leather goods companies such as Hermès buying their own farms.

SPECIAL STAMPS

The 'shooting star' stamp was reserved for Hermès artisans producing a bag for their own personal use. They were entitled to make one bag a year. Today, the shooting star has been replaced by a number under the logo stamp.

'Special' Hermès stamps include the 'horseshoe' symbol used for special orders or so-called 'à la carte' bags. Within certain guidelines set out by the brand, customers can choose the leather, colour, shade of stitching and metal hardware of their bag. Two-colour or three-colour bags are also an option. The production time is six months to a year. A bag with this stamp has therefore been created by a customer lucky enough to order a bespoke bag.

DATE CODES

Ⓐ	Ⓑ	Ⓒ	Ⓓ	Ⓔ	Ⓕ	Ⓖ
1971	1972	1973	1974	1975	1976	1977
Ⓗ	Ⓘ	Ⓙ	Ⓚ	Ⓛ	Ⓜ	Ⓝ
1978	1979	1980	1981	1982	1983	1984
Ⓞ	Ⓟ	Ⓠ	Ⓡ	Ⓢ	Ⓣ	Ⓤ
1985	1986	1987	1988	1989	1990	1991
Ⓥ	Ⓦ	Ⓧ	Ⓨ	Ⓩ		
1992	1993	1994	1995	1996		

A	B	C	D	E	F
1997	1998	1999	2000	2001	2002
G	H	I	J	K	L
2003	2004	2005	2006	2007	2008
M	N	O	P	Q	R
2009	2010	2011	2012	2013	2014

T	X	A	C	D
2015	2016	2017	2018	2019
Y	Z	U	B	W
2020	2021	2022	2023	2024

LOGO STAMPS

- The logo stamp 'Hermès Paris 24 Fbg St Honoré' was used by Hermès from 1930 to 1949.
- The logo stamp 'Hermès Paris' on a single line was used from 1950 to 1970.
- The logo stamp 'Hermès Paris' over two lines was used from 1965 to 1970.
- The logo stamp 'Hermès Paris Made in France' has been used by the fashion house since 1971.

THE KELLY

BY HERMÈS

Considered the iconic Hermès bag, the Kelly is as young as ever despite its origins dating back to the 1930s. Designed by Robert Dumas, it was initially called the Sac de voyage à courroies pour dame *(ladies' travel bag with straps).*

THREE TYPES OF LEATHER

The bag was originally made from the following leathers: box calf (the brand's famous signature smooth leather), pigskin (unlike the fragile box calf, this leather is extremely hard-wearing) and crocodile skin.

BIRTH OF AN ICONIC BAG

In 1956, Grace, Princess of Monaco (the former Grace Kelly), gave the bag her royal seal of approval. In April, she was photographed for *Life* magazine holding the bag in front of her to hide her pregnancy. That same year, the young princess ordered several variations of the model, which at the time was called *Petit sac haut, fermeture à courroies et cadenas* (small high bag with strap closure and lock).

It immediately became a worldwide success, with the bag now symbolizing the dream of the American actor who came to marry a European prince. To celebrate this triumph, Hermès decided to give the bag the name we know it by today: the Kelly.

A RARE AND HIGHLY SOUGHT-AFTER PIECE

The success of the Kelly has continued undimmed, despite the advent of its cousin, the Birkin bag, created in the 1980s. For almost 70 years, the Kelly has continued to be the best-selling iconic bag in the luxury goods market. With the passing decades and as demand continued to increase, in the 1990s Hermès introduced a quota system and waiting list in an effort to control the bag's image and production times: supply was restricted to accentuate its desirability, resulting in an aura of rarity around the piece.

On the contemporary pre-owned market, Kelly bags in excellent condition are even being resold for more than their current retail value. With the Birkin and the Constance, it is among the three most sought-after Hermès bags.

Princess Grace and Prince Rainier,
Philadelphia, 5 January 1956.

The young princess ordered several variations of the Petit sac haut, fermeture à courroies et cadenas *(small high bag with strap closure and lock).*

ANATOMY OF THE KELLY BAG

It has:
• one handle
• a trapezoid shape
• a flap closed by two side straps and fastened with a turnlock clasp.

Handle

D-ring or
double D-ring

Chape
(*enchape*)

Leather tie (*tirette*)

Turnlock clasp
(*touret*)

Side strap (*sanglon*)

Bell lanyard
(*clochette*)

Lock

THE ORIGIN OF BOX CALF
Box calf leather is sometimes said to be named after Joseph
Box, a famous London shoemaker of the early 20th century.

THE HERMÈS LOGO STAMP

The logo stamp 'Hermès Paris Made in France' first appeared in 1971. Prior to this date, bags were stamped 'Hermès Paris' or 'Hermès Paris 24 Fbg St Honoré'.

RECOGNIZABLE FINISHES

THE KELLY SELLIER

The Kelly Sellier bag has a saddlemaker (*sellier*) finish, and its boxy silhouette features clean lines and crisp edges to emphasize its classic trapezoid shape. The visible seams highlight the outstanding quality of craftsmanship required to make the bag. Each end of the bag features a firm, non-flexible fold to create the rigid structure.

THE KELLY RETOURNÉ

In comparison, the Kelly Retourné offers a more relaxed aesthetic. The bag is turned inside out to reveal the interior seams, which are then covered with piping. The leather of the bag is generally suppler, giving it a softly curved appearance. The Kelly Retourné does not have the same fold as the Sellier at the ends, allowing the sides of the bag to move farther apart to create a different silhouette.

KELLY SIZES

The first sizes produced by Hermès were 28 and 32cm. Other sizes have been released over the years: 20 (or Mini Kelly), 25, 35 and 40cm. Today, the bag is made in eight sizes: 15, 20, 25, 28, 32, 35, 40 and 50cm.

Kelly 25
25 × 17 × 10.5cm

Kelly 28
28 × 22 × 11.5cm

Kelly 32
32 × 23 × 12cm

Kelly 35
35 × 25 × 13cm

ICONIC ITERATIONS

In 1960, Hermès released a canvas and leather version for the first time. Available in both the Sellier and Retourné styles, this option was introduced at the request of the brand's customers. At that time, the closures were gold-plated. It was not until the 1990s that silver-tone palladium plating was used.

In 1983, the first three-colour Kelly was released, crafted in green, red and blue box leather. This was quickly followed by other colour variations and an exotic leather version.

In 2000, Jean-Louis Dumas designed a playful version of the Kelly known as the Kelly Doll, produced in eight different colours. At the time, this small 17cm bag was retailed by the fashion house at a price of £1,500/$2,300; today, its resale value can be as high as £60,000/$75,000. Other versions were released from 2008 onwards.

For his first collection as creative director at Hermès, Jean Paul Gaultier released a flattened version of the Kelly known as the Kelly Shoulder for his Autumn/ Winter 2004/05 show. From 2004 to 2011, the designer was head of couture creations for the fashion house, developing many sought-after limited series.

Released in 2010, one of the most successful series was undoubtedly the So Black collection featuring smooth leather and black hardware. This was the first time that Hermès had changed the colour of its packaging for a collection: the box for the bag was black, as was the dustbag.

Still under the leadership of Gaultier, the Kelly Flat was released for the Spring/Summer 2007 collection. Worn with a tied shoulder strap and folded in half on the arms of the models, the bag was made from Swift or Barenia calfskin and designed for the first time without a turnlock, instead fastening with an Étrivière (stirrup) buckle strap that looped back on itself. This was one of the supplest versions of the Kelly made by the fashion house. The shoulder strap attaches to the D-rings in the style of a belt.

THE BIRKIN

Once upon a time there was the Birkin – a bag born in 1984 on a plane. At least, that is the story surrounding the creation of this iconic bag. On a flight from Paris to London, Jean-Louis Dumas, who had been head of Hermès since 1978, met the already famous Jane Birkin. The singer was despairing at not being able to find a bag practical or big enough for her life as a young mother, and was known for her trademark hefty wicker baskets.

THE LEGENDARY STORY OF AN ICONIC BAG

As Jane Birkin's belongings fell from her bag on to the floor, Jean-Louis Dumas advised her, 'You should get one with pockets,' to which she retorted with her usual panache: 'The day Hermès makes one with pockets, I'll have that.' He then let her know who he was: 'But I *am* Hermès.' The young mother, who had just given birth to Charlotte Gainsbourg, seized the opportunity and asked him why the leather goods maker could not design a bag four times bigger than the Kelly but smaller than Serge Gainsbourg's iconic suitcase.

So the CEO of Hermès decided to use the basic structure of a pre-existing bag known as the *Haut à Courroies*, adapting it to create a handbag. This is how – so the tale goes – the Birkin bag was born in 1984.

A RANGE OF SIZES

When it was launched, the Birkin came in only one size of 32cm. The *pontets*, or strap guides, were open at the bottom and not at the top as they are on today's bags. The bag is currently made in almost every size: 20, 25, 30, 35, 40, 45 and 50cm.

THE MOST DESIRABLE BAG IN THE WORLD

The Birkin is considered to be one of the most sought-after bags in the world. It takes almost forty hours' work to craft what must be the holy grail of any wardrobe. In its exotic leather versions, it holds the record for the most expensive pre-owned bag sold at auction: a Himalaya Crocodile Diamond Birkin went for $450,000 (£336,000) at Sotheby's in 2022.

Handle

Turnlock clasp (*touret*)

Strap guide
(*pontet*)

Side strap
(*sanglon*)

Chape
(*enchape*)

With a trapezoid shape, the Birkin has two handles and a cut-out flap,
closed by two side straps resting on strap guides
and fastened with a turnlock clasp.

Jane Birkin in
1985 carrying
the bag she
helped bring
into the world.

THE SADDLE STITCH

A signature technique at Hermès is the saddle, or *sellier*, stitch that is sewn by hand. However, Hermès bags are far from being entirely hand-sewn: on a Birkin or Kelly, it is estimated that 15 per cent of all stitching is done by hand and the rest is machine sewn (which takes nothing away from the quality of the finished product).

The key feature of the saddle stitch is its strength: two needles are required when sewing it by hand, each one crossing over the other at every stitch, so that, if one of the threads breaks, the seam does not entirely unravel.

How did the 'saddle stitch' get its name? Simply because this type of seam originated in the equestrian world. It is used not only to make saddles but also in other applications such as automotive upholstery.

BIRKIN SIZES

Birkin 25
25 × 20 × 13cm

Birkin 30
30 × 22 × 16cm

Birkin 35
35 × 25 × 18cm

Birkin 40
40 × 30 × 21cm

ICONIC ITERATIONS

Like its cousin the Kelly, the Shoulder Birkin was designed by Jean Paul Gaultier for his Autumn/Winter 2004/05 runway show. This model fell out of favour due to its bulky, impractical nature and visually unappealing looks.

The Shadow Birkin presented in the Autumn/Winter 2009/10 collection was an immediate success. In this technical feat of craftsmanship, all the elements of the bag are embossed in a trompe-l'oeil effect including the flap, *sanglons* and *clochette*.

In 2011, the Ghillies Birkin offered a British Isles version of the bag. It features perforations inspired by the shoes worn for Irish and Scottish folk dancing.

A BAG WITHOUT A SHOULDER STRAP

With the exception of the Tiny Birkin released in 2011, and an unpromising test run by the fashion house when the original was first launched, the Birkin cannot be worn across the shoulder. Today, Hermès offers 'harness straps' allowing shoulder wear, but – for the time being at least – the model cannot be worn on the shoulder without using some kind of additional system.

THE HAUT À COURROIES

BY HERMÈS

In 1892, the Haut à Courroies, or HAC, was the first bag to be made by Hermès. It was not a handbag in the true sense of the word but a large pouch designed to hold a pair of riding boots and a saddle. This was an unsurprising development, given that Hermès originally created equestrian equipment. At the time, Émile Maurice Hermès, grandson of the founder, noticed on one of his trips abroad that Argentinian cattle ranchers stored their saddles in a flexible trapezoid shaped bag.

THE FIRST HAC BAGS

This bag for saddles was created in the late-19th century and, without its makers knowing it, laid the foundations for both the Kelly and Birkin bags. In 1958, it was renamed the Haut à Courroies, or HAC. Between its creation at the end of the 19th century and 1958, it was known by different names and produced in multiple variations.

PRECISE SPECIFICATIONS

The first releases of the HAC were available in 40, 45, 50, 55 and 60cm sizes suitable for a travel bag. The spindle of the *touret* is unusual in that it has a square tip, unlike the round tips on the Birkin and Kelly.

Square turnlock clasp (touret) on the Haut à Courroies bag.

TWO TYPES OF FINISH

Now thought of as the Birkin for men, the Haut à Courroies comes in various sizes that are more suited to its use as a smaller bag: 32, 35, 40, 45, 50 and 55cm. The closure system varies: some bags have the rounded *touret* of the Birkin and Kelly while others have retained the unique square tip.

Handles

Turnlock clasp (*touret*)

Side strap (*sanglon*)

Lock

Strap guide on pad (*pontet sur patin*)

Leather tie (*tirette*)

Bell lanyard (*clochette*)

HERE IS THE HAC!

In the 1983 film *Circulez y'a rien à voir!* by Patrice Leconte, Jane Birkin wears an HAC bag. In sporting the Birkin's cousin on the big screen, she was unknowingly anticipating the chance mid-air meeting she would have a year later with Jean-Louis Dumas, then CEO of Hermès, that would result in the Birkin.

Two versions of the HAC

This 1993 model measures 32cm along the base and is inspired by the 1924 version, the year the first HAC was released in canvas and leather with reinforced corners. It is shown here in a Toile H canvas and Barenia calfskin variant.

This 2019 model is from the brand's menswear department. The 40cm size is the perfect roomy bag for daily use and is also popular as a travel bag.

TOP-HANDLE BAGS

BY HERMÈS

Hermès bags from the 1940s and 1960s are rare and highly sought-after pieces. They share the common feature of being handheld. Rectangular in shape, they have a metal clasp and rigid handle.

TO EACH BAG ITS CLASP

These bags are often made from box calf or, in the more luxurious versions, more exotic leathers, while the interior is lined with beautifully soft lambskin. The interior of the bag has two gussets and a slip pocket fastened with a press stud to hold a small mirror sold with the bag. Today, these are true collector's items: as the years pass, it is becoming relatively rare to find them in very good condition. Although they all have similar shapes, the differentiating feature is often the clasp, the shape of which often provides a clue to the name of the bag.

BAGS TURNED HERMÈS ICONS

Somewhat overlooked in recent decades, probably because they lack a long strap to carry them on the shoulder or crossbody, top-handle bags are now particularly appreciated by international customers looking for timeless and classic Hermès pieces.

ICONIC ITERATIONS

Princesse bag created in the 1950s, in black suede reindeer leather. If in excellent condition, this bag is a highly prized collector's item as its leather is extremely delicate.

Mumm Champagne bag created in 1994 for the champagne producer Mumm. The interior of the bag features the green and red signature colours of the famous Reims champagne. The handle is held in place with two metal parts replicating champagne corks, and the bag was sold with a small torch.

Iconic Chaîne d'ancre bags from the 1960s, in three different leathers: black crocodile, black box and brown lizard.

Cordeau or Cordelière bag in dark-brown *porosus* crocodile, created in the 1960s.

Demi-lune bag, released in the 1970s in brown alligator leather and gold-tone hardware, with gold-tone swivel clasp.

Piano bag in canvas and leather. Combined use of these two materials is typical of the fashion house. This blend of canvas and leather lightens the weight of the bag and creates a more casual look.

Ring bag in leather and crinoline, created in the 1970s. Crinoline, a durable fibre formed from woven horsehair, is a material widely used by Hermès in the production of vintage bags and connects with its equestrian heritage.

Escale bag in pangolin leather, created in the 1960s. It is probably the rarest of the Hermès top-handle bags. Production of this type of leather was not common at the time, making this model a real collector's item.

Étrier bag in peccary leather, created in the 1960s. The name of the bag comes from the shape of its clasp, which is reminiscent of a riding stirrup (*étrier*). Although highly durable, peccary leather is no longer used as it is made from pig skin, which is felt to be inappropriate for the world of luxury goods.

Boutonnière bag in black box leather, created in the 1960s.

HERMÈS CLASPS

Top-handle bags would evolve into shoulder bags, such as this Sandrine bag in box leather featuring a shoulder strap with a choice of two different positions.

THE CONSTANCE

BY HERMÈS

The Constance bag has a shorter history than its cousins, the Kelly and the Birkin. Despite its resolutely modern lines, this piece dates back to 1967 when Jean Louis Dumas asked the designer Catherine Chaillet to create a bag for Hermès. She was pregnant at the time and so designed a bag to suit her situation: highly practical, and wearable on the shoulder or crossbody.

NEWBORN AT HERMÈS

Legend has it that the designer gave birth on the day the bag was launched, hence the name of Constance, which is what she called her daughter. It is fitting that the bag embodies one of the values most cherished by Hermès: the concept of transmission down the generations, including from mother to daughter.

A BREAK WITH HERMÈS TRADITION

Requiring around 16 hours of craftsmanship, this bag is a technical feat and one of the most difficult models to produce. Universally recognizable on its release thanks to the imposing gold-plated H clasp, it was produced in a wide variety of finishes.

Unlike the Bolide representing the 'quiet luxury' trend, the Constance was the first Hermès bag to feature a visible logo. Its interior lining is made from soft and sensual lambskin, and the larger versions of the bag have an interior zip.

AN ARCHITECTURAL CLASP

The H was a clever first, acting as an ingenious and functional clasp. It opens and closes via a spring mechanism concealed at either end of the bar attached to the flap. Well balanced and standing firmly on its two feet with an intersecting horizontal bar, this H-shaped clasp is pleasingly uniform and harmonious.

'Luxury is rarity, creativity, elegance.'

Pierre Cardin

A SHOULDER STRAP BAG

The shoulder strap is sewn into the body of the bag and cannot be removed; its length can be changed by pulling the strap through the two attachments fixed to the top of the bag. The Constance is available in several sizes: the Micro is 15cm, the Mini 18cm and the Classique 24cm. There are also so-called 'vintage' sizes in 23, 25 and 29cm.

CONSTANCE SIZES

← 15cm →

← 18cm →

← 24cm →

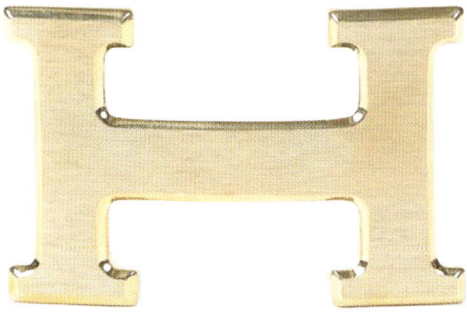

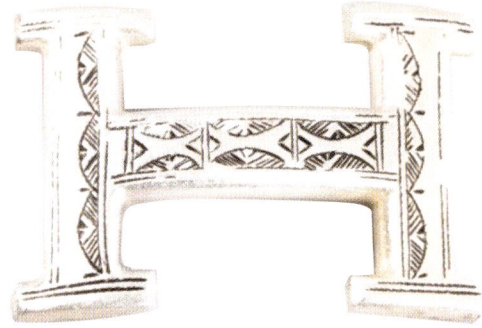

With the dazzling success of the bag, the fashion house quickly released a belt buckle, also known as the Constance, to replicate the iconic clasp. At the time, it was the best-selling Hermès buckle.

Shown here in its 'Touareg' version in chased S925 silver, the Constance buckle is available in many different sizes and finishes.

Constance bag in Rouge H box calf leather and Toile H canvas, with H clasp in silver-tone palladium, 2002.

THE ÉVELYNE

BY HERMÈS

In 1978, Évelyne Bertrand, head of the Hermès riding department, gave her name to the bag she designed. Riders who were regular customers of the fashion house had asked her to create a practical bag for carrying grooming essentials, such as brushes, curry combs and hoof picks.

HORSESHOE

The design of the Évelyne is simple: a horseshoe-shaped bag with an unlined interior and no interior pockets. The bag is closed with a press-stud leather tab decorated with a saddle-nail motif, and carried using a canvas shoulder strap. On one side, 63 perforations in the form of a hoofprint around the letter H allow air into the bag to dry grooming brushes. The logo, nowadays worn facing outwards, was originally meant to be worn against the body.

AN ULTRA-PRACTICAL BAG

Designed for the equestrian community, Hermès never planned for the Évelyne to become a handbag. However, its practicality meant that it was quickly diverted from its original purpose – the wide, comfortable canvas strap made it the perfect everyday choice for active women.

SEVERAL DIFFERENT MODELS

The Évelyne bag is available in three versions. The 'Évelyne I' is the first generation and does not have an exterior pocket or adjustable shoulder strap. As its name suggests, the 'Évelyne II' is the second generation: it has an exterior pocket but the shoulder strap is still not adjustable. The 'Évelyne III' comes with an exterior pocket and an adjustable shoulder strap.

The bag is available in four sizes: TPM (*Très Petit Modèle*, or Mini), PM (*Petit Modèle*, or Small), GM (*Grand Modèle*, or Large) and TGM (*Très Grand Modèle*, or Very Large).

THE MOST AFFORDABLE HERMÈS BAG
Although the Évelyne was created at the end of the 1970s, it was not until 2009 and the global economic recession that the popularity of the model took off. It has one of the lowest Hermès price points, with resale pieces selling for around £1,600/$2,000.

ÉVELYNE SIZES

TPM
16 × 18 × 5cm

PM
29 × 30 × 8cm

GM
33 × 31 × 8cm

TGM
40 × 44 × 10cm

ICONIC ITERATIONS

Variations of the model in canvas and leather.

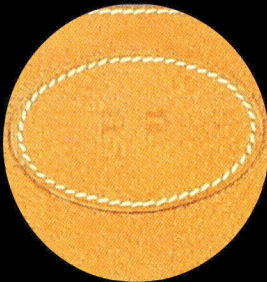

QUIET LUXURY
The Bolide features an oval badge on the front side for the application of customized monograms. As one of the most discreet and understated bags produced by Hermès, this design fits most neatly into the 'quiet luxury' trend, with no visible logo or other distinguishing marks.

THE BOLIDE

BY HERMÈS

After the first steps taken by Thierry Hermès into the world of fashion, the illustrious empire run by his sons continued to create masterpieces for the most fortunate in society. When his grandson Émile-Maurice Hermès visited Henry Ford's pioneering automobile factory, he discovered an ingenious device that would soon transform the world of fashion: the zip fastener. A few years later, driven by a spirit of innovation, the company filed a patent to protect its bold idea of incorporating the revolutionary zip fastener into its bags.

AN IDEAL TRAVEL BAG

In 1923, the *Sac pour l'auto*, or Car bag (the original name of the Bolide), was the first bag in the world to be fitted with a zip. Designed solely as a travel bag, the zip closure guaranteed that its contents would stay safely inside, ensuring a stress-free travel experience for its owners. The rounded shape also meant that it could easily be slipped into the boot/trunk of the cars of the period, and two solid handles made it easy to carry and transport.

FROM BUGATTI TO BOLIDE

In 1925, the original bag was renamed the Bugatti as a tribute to Ettore Bugatti, the famous car manufacturer who is thought to have been the first person to order the bag from Hermès.

After an interruption in production, the fashion house returned the bag to its collection in 1983 and renamed it the Bolide in 1995. That same year, Hermès was ordered to pay 300,000 francs (£40,000/$60,000) in damages to Bugatti International for using its name without its agreement.

TWO LINES

Two lines were created for the bag:
• the original line has four sizes: the Bolide 27, Bolide 31, Bolide 35 and Bolide 45.
• the Bolide 1923 line offers a version of the bag without the oval badge; it is available in Mini, Bolide 25 and Bolide 30 sizes. The Bolide Mini is the only model without keys or a lock.

LEATHERS

As the fashion house has a vast range of leathers at its disposal, the Bolide bag is available in several standard leathers:
• Clemence leather is matt, flat-grained and scratch-resistant, making it a hard-wearing option.
• For a lighter feel, Epsom leather is an embossed calfskin that has a more rigid grain than Clemence leather.
• Sikkim is a lesser-known leather but is as soft as velvet. It has little or no grain, and because it is relatively thin and lightweight, it creates a relaxed 'slouchy' effect.

BOLIDE SIZES

Bolide 1923 Mini
20 × 15 × 8cm

Bolide 1923 25
25 × 20 × 11cm

Bolide 27
27 × 25 × 10cm

Bolide 1923 30
30 × 23 × 13cm

Bolide 45
45 × 35 × 24cm

Originally designed as a travel bag for men, the Bolide is now worn primarily as a women's handbag. For the menswear Autumn/Winter 2016 collection, artistic director Véronique Nichanian designed a fun version known as the Bolide Shark.

The Bolide 1923 Sportif, menswear Spring/Summer 2018 collection, with dark-red baseball stitching on a grey body. Perfect as a gym bag or travel bag with a hint of adventure.

CHANEL
FAJHION CODEJ AND PRINCIPLEJ

Thanks to her strong identity and longevity as the head of design, Gabrielle Chanel continues to be inseparable from the fashion house she created. A rare phenomenon today, the House of Chanel is recognized not only for its leather goods but also for its now-iconic haute couture pieces.

A CHILDHOOD SHROUDED IN MYSTERY

Gabrielle Chanel was born in Saumur, Marne-et-Loire, on 19 August 1883. It is worth noting that she was born under the star sign Leo, as the lion motif would play an important role in her collections, used on suit buttons, ornaments and so on. Otherwise, very little is known about her childhood, as the woman who would later be known simply as Mademoiselle was always keen to surround her personal life with myth and mystery.

The most popular version of her start in life is the one we will use here: she was abandoned by her father at the convent of Aubazine in the department of Corrèze. The importance of her life in the orphanage should not be underestimated and would inform key elements of her style: her use of clean lines, black-and-white colour schemes, and her chain belts replicating those of the nuns.

WHY THE NAME 'COCO'?

At the age of 18, Gabrielle Chanel went to live with her aunt in Moulins in the department of Allier. Here she tried her hand at singing as a *poseuse* (a performer who entertained the crowd between star turns) at the café-concert La Rotonde. Her repertoire included the song 'Qui qu'a vu Coco dans l'Trocadéro'. She was cheered on by the public with loud chants of 'Coco', and the nickname stuck. It was here that she met the socialite Étienne Balsan who, after chanting her nickname, suggested she came to live with him in Compiègne, a town some 70km north-east of Paris.

GIVING FASHION CODES A RADICAL TWIST

It was through her contact with Balsan at the beginning of the 20th century that the woman now known as Coco Chanel became familiar with the fashion codes and rules of high society. Starting out in her career as a milliner, she created her first hat designs for Émilienne Alençon, a famous courtesan. It was also at this time that she began to joyously appropriate the male wardrobe by taking her lover's riding clothes and adapting them so she could wear them herself.

> ## 'She has the best-dressed body and soul on Earth.' Salvador Dalí

FIRST STEPS IN FASHION

In 1910, Chanel opened a hat shop known as Chanel Modes at 21 rue Cambon in Paris. Her company enjoyed immediate success, rapidly becoming a firm favourite with famous female actors. As a dressmaker was already working in the adjacent premises, the commercial lease prohibited Gabrielle Chanel from selling clothes.

In 1913, Chanel's lover the English polo player Boy Capel financed the opening of a boutique in the seaside resort of Deauville, Normandy. When war broke out in 1914, wealthy Parisians fleeing the capital often paid a visit to the fashion designer. Having understood the opportunity offered by holiday resorts, Chanel opened another boutique in Biarritz in 1915. In the Autumn/Winter 1916 season, she presented her first complete couture collection.

THE DARK YEARS

At the end of the First World War, Mademoiselle started to market the perfume Chanel No. 5 created by Ernest Beaux, a famous perfumer. In 1924, following the success of the fragrance and for financial reasons, the Wertheimer brothers (then owners of perfume house Bourjois) entered into a contract with the designer, granting her 10 per cent of the stock of Parfums Chanel. During the Second World War, the fashion house closed its doors (making 4,000 employees redundant), and only perfumes and accessories continued to be sold. After the end of the war, suspected friendships with the occupying Nazis forced Gabrielle into voluntary exile in Switzerland for ten years.

A TRIBUTE

Bouquet de Catherine was the name given to the 'recipe' for No. 5 before it became the must-have perfume of the House of Chanel. Ernest Beaux created the perfume in Moscow in homage to Catherine the Great and the tercentenary of the founding of the Romanov dynasty. It proved a failure, but would find success ten years later thanks to Mademoiselle (and to Marilyn Monroe who, after all, wore nothing more than a few drops of No. 5 in bed!).

SIMPLICITY AND PRACTICALITY

From her Swiss retreat, Gabrielle Chanel witnessed Christian Dior's 'explosive' New Look, which went completely against her vision of fashion. She therefore decided to return to Paris to restore the rules she believed fashion should live by – in other words, simplicity and practicality. Legend has it that, during a copious meal with Boy Capel, her corset came undone and the designer swore that she would never wear restrictive clothing again. She wanted to see women enjoy the same privileges as men: to be dressed comfortably while remaining stylish. She was completely opposed to the designs of Dior, which she considered too oppressive and too restrictive for women, likening them to costumes.

Illustration from French fashion journal *Les Élégances parisiennes: publication officielle des industries françaises de la mode*, 1916.

Actor Jacqueline Forzane buying a hat from Gabrielle Chanel in her Deauville boutique. Lithograph by Sem, 1919.

The couture house was reopened in 1954. Although rejected by the European press, the brand enjoyed immense success in the United States. The modern American woman felt that she had been understood, thanks to accessories allowing her to adapt the tone of an outfit over the course of the day, meaning she no longer had to change in the evening. For example, by pinning an ornate brooch to her suit, it could be made perfect for eveningwear, too. That same year, 1954, Chanel SA was created: the firm Chanel Parfums bought Chanel Couture, and the Wertheimer brothers bought the entire operation from Mademoiselle, on condition that she remained in charge and was granted certain privileges.

Revolution was in the air with the advent of ready-to-wear. Categorically refusing to allow it into her fashion house, she marketed these collections through a series of licences. This arrangement would continue until her death in 1971.

A BREATH OF FRESH AIR – WITH RESPECT FOR TRADITION

It was not until Karl Lagerfeld joined Chanel as creative director in 1983 that the fashion house rediscovered the dazzling success of its past. An outstanding creative genius, he lost no time in analysing the DNA of the fashion house (pearls, camellias, chains, the quilted motif, and iconic materials such as tweed and jersey) and reinterpreting it with a modern twist. These signature elements were also transposed on to leather goods and accessories, reaching the height of their popularity in the 1980s. For example, Mademoiselle created the famous 2.55 bag in 1955, and Karl would draw the shapes of the famous Classic Flap bag in 1983.

LEATHERS

The signature leather of Chanel is lambskin. It is supple, fine and light, and particularly soft to the touch. The diamond-shaped quilting on the fashion house's iconic bags - a reference to the jackets worn by stableboys - was created with machine stitching. Lambskin leather is particularly prone to scratches and scuffs.

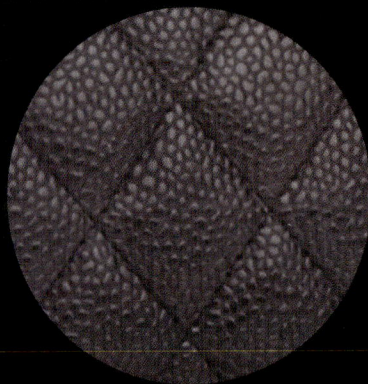

The leather known as 'caviar' is a grained calfskin. It is the second most iconic Chanel leather. First used in the 1980s, it has undergone many transformations before becoming the leather we know today. It is used for day bags and, unlike lambskin, is very hard-wearing.

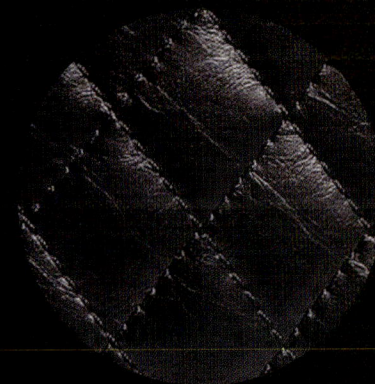

Aged calfskin has been used since 2005. To mark the fiftieth anniversary of the 2.55 bag, Karl Lagerfeld offered a modernized version known as the 2.55 Reissue.

FABRICS

Chanel has been working with jersey since 1913. At the time, this simple, machine-knitted fabric was used only for men's underwear and naval clothing. Its name comes from the island of Jersey off the Normandy coast. When transposed on to dresses and suits, the material hugged the body, marking a revolutionary turning point in the history of fashion. Originally made from wool, today it can also be made from cotton or synthetic materials. Once established as an iconic fabric of the fashion house, jersey quickly became a staple material in leather goods despite its fragility.

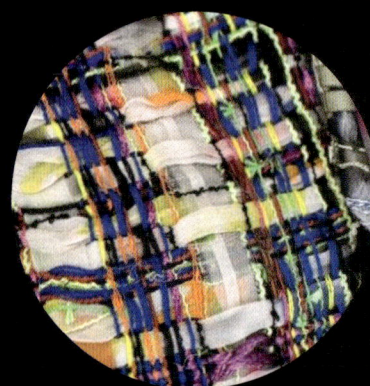

Alongside jersey, tweed is the other signature fabric of Chanel. During her relationship with the 2nd Duke of Westminster, Mademoiselle formed a special bond with tweed. This quintessential British fabric could be seen as a symbol of their love story. When Karl Lagerfeld arrived in 1983, he used tweed in a way that respected the heritage of Chanel while reusing its fashion codes. It was not until the early 1990s that tweed was set free from its understated past.

DATE CODES

Date codes were introduced at Chanel in 1986 in the form of stickers known as holograms. These stickers are duplicated with an authenticity card showing the same number. In 2021, the hologram was replaced by a microchip and engraving on a metal plate or a sticker on certain types of leather goods.

On the holograms, only the first two digits are useful for dating a piece. Until the beginning of 2005, the code consisted of seven digits. After this date, the code was expanded to eight digits.

SERIAL NUMBERS	YEAR	SERIAL NUMBERS	YEAR
30XXXXXX	2020	14XXXXX	2011
29XXXXXX	2019	13XXXXX	2009-10
28XXXXXX	2019	12XXXXX	2008-9
27XXXXXX	2019	11XXXXX	2006-7
26XXXXXX	2018-19	10XXXXXX	2005-6
25XXXXXX	2018	9XXXXXX	2004-5
24XXXXXX	2017-18	8XXXXX	2003-4
23XXXXXX	2016-17	7XXXXX	2002-3
22XXXXXX	2016	6XXXXX	2000-2
21XXXXXX	2015-16	5XXXXX	1997-9
20XXXXXX	2014-15	4XXXXX	1996-7
19XXXXXX	2014	3XXXXX	1994-5
18XXXXXX	2013-14	2XXXXX	1991-4
17XXXXXX	2012-13	1XXXXXX	1989-91
16XXXXXX	2012	0XXXXX	1986-8
15XXXXXX	2011-12		

THE 2.55

Setting women free of the constraints imposed on them by society was a cause close to Gabrielle Chanel's heart. After taking on the corset and dresses that restricted natural movement, she turned her attention to the handbag. Models from the late 19th century were worn in the crook of the arm and prevented women from having their hands free.

FREEDOM FIRST AND FOREMOST

In 1929, Gabrielle Chanel designed her first model of a shoulder bag, which was directly inspired by the straps on military packs and was a distant version of the bag she would create 26 years later in 1955.

As in perfumery, Mademoiselle liked to give her designs numbers. Launched in February 1955, the bag was named the 2.55. An icon was born. The couturière's love of fabrics led her to create three versions of the bag: one in quilted lambskin for daytime, and two versions for the evening, one in jersey and the other in satin.

'She knows that personality is expressed through the accessory.'
Elizabeth, Princess Bibesco, 1928

UNIQUE KNOW-HOW

The body of the 2.55 is rectangular and has a double flap closed with a swivel turnlock clasp known as the Mademoiselle. The chased chain is adjustable in length and reminiscent of the belts worn by the nuns at the Aubazine orphanage where the designer grew up. It is known as the Signature or Cambon chain. The bag is quilted, evoking the jackets worn by stableboys on racecourses and the saddle pads of horses. The interior lining is in burgundy leather or ottoman and recalls the colour of the uniforms worn by the residents of the orphanage. The Chanel logo is stitched on the inner flap and sits above the stamp of the fashion house.

The bag has a total of seven pockets. The exterior one on the back is known as the Mona Lisa Smile because of its shallow crescent shape. The other six are in the interior. One is a tubular pocket designed to hold lipstick (which Mademoiselle made popular again after the First World War). Two others, on either side of the lipstick pocket, are bellows pockets and can be used for business cards or powder compacts (a credit card holder was introduced in 1965, the year in which women in France could finally manage their financial affairs entirely independently). The pocket called the Secret is zipped and located under the flap – a feature used by the couturière to hide her lovers' letters. The last two pockets are large and can be used to store letters and documents. No fewer than 180 processes and up to 15 hours' work are required to create this model.

AN EXEMPLARY DECISION

In 2019, the House of Chanel decided to stop manufacturing bags made from exotic skins. Citing the complex traceability of the leather supply chain, the fashion house preferred to discontinue this type of product.

Signature
chain strap

Mademoiselle clasp

Pocket known as
the Mona Lisa Smile

2.55 SIZES

In the 1990s, sales of the 2.55 lost momentum following the launch of the Classic Flap bag. This resulted in Karl Lagerfeld designing a modernized version known as the 2.55 Reissue. It was launched in 2005 to mark the fiftieth anniversary of the iconic model, and modifications were introduced to the original design. An additional aged calfskin leather was available for this model, and metal finishes were no longer offered only in gold but also in ruthenium and champagne. Today, the 2.55 is still a must-have bag and is reinterpreted in almost every collection of the fashion house.

Small (224)

←——— 20cm ———→

Medium (225)

←——— 24cm ———→

Large (226)

←——— 28cm ———→

Maxi (227)

←——— 31cm ———→

ICONIC ITERATIONS

Version of the famous 2.55 bag from the Autumn/Winter 2007 ready-to-wear collection, made from fringed wool with a multi-coloured check pattern and beads. This model was worn by Louise, Carrie Bradshaw's assistant, in the 2008 film *Sex and the City*.

The 2.55 'Lucky Charm' is one of the most successful versions of the bag. As a result, several variations have been marketed in different collections.

Variation of the 2009 2.55 'Messenger' model. Entirely covered in gold sequins, it has an adjustable shoulder strap in beige leather.

The 2.55 Reissue in black quilted and aged calfskin, with clasp and handle in antique gold. Historic finish with double flap.

Also from the Autumn/Winter 2007 collection, this model is in vermilion silk topstitched with a crocodile-style pattern and gold-tone hardware.

This 1960s model features an interlaced chain rather than the traditional Signature version. As production at the time was not standardized as it is today, certain variations were released at the request of the fashion house or the customer.

THE CLASSIC FLAP

BY CHANEL

We will refer to it here as the Classic Flap bag, although it is also known as the Timeless or 11.12. Today, all three names are used for the same model. The year 1983 marked a turning point in the history of Chanel: designer Karl Lagerfeld was appointed creative director, and praise for the brand's latest star bag was off the scale. Although the foundations of the 11.12 bag were laid in 1973, it was not until 1983 that it adopted its final form.

CONSTANTLY EVOLVING HARDWARE

Since the first CC clasps were designed, many different forms were tried and tested before the definitive versions we know today emerged. For example, in the closure known as the 'duckbill', the turnlock was flattened to resemble the end of a flat screwdriver. In another version, the CC clasp was placed on a press stud.

THE CLASP AND CHAIN

In terms of the technical specifications of the bag, they were almost identical to those of the 2.55, including the number of pockets and the double-flap system. In other respects, there were big differences: the CC clasp replaced the Mademoiselle closure, and a chain interwoven with leather was used instead of the Signature chain. The CC clasp was plated in 24-carat gold from the launch of the bag until 2008, at which point Chanel opted for a simple gold-tone finish instead. For bags made in France, a hallmark on the clasp can be used to authenticate this gold plating, although it may not be present on bags made in Italy. Contrary to popular belief, the metal parts of the bag are not made of solid gold but only plated.

CC turnlock clasp   Chain interwoven with leather

Pocket known as the Mona Lisa Smile

Lining in bordeaux leather

CC stitched under the flap

Press-stud closure on the inner flap

IDENTIFYING A CHANEL BAG

The lower left part of the CC clasp always overlaps the lower right part where they intersect, and this position is reversed at the upper intersection. One important detail for authenticating a Chanel Classic Flap bag is that, on a small production run made in the early 1980s, the direction may be reversed. However, once the base specification of the Classic Flap had been definitively established, there were no other variations.

HIGHLY IDENTIFIABLE SIZES

The Classic Flap comes in many different finishes: lambskin, caviar grained calfskin, jersey, tweed, exotic skins and PVC. With each collection, Karl Lagerfeld rose to the challenge of embracing inventiveness and ingenuity, ensuring that models would become highly collectible.

Added to this are the different sizes of the bag, the smallest being the Extra Mini. This is followed by the Mini, Small, Medium, Jumbo and Maxi Jumbo sizes. The way all these pieces are worn is different, as some can only be handheld or worn on the shoulder, while others can also be worn crossbody. The oldest models can rarely be worn crossbody. Both the 2.55 and Classic Flap bags can have either a single flap or a double flap. The simplified variation of a single flap was discontinued in 2014, the fashion house deciding that it had moved too far away from the original model.

While the 2.55 is distinguished by its refined, discreet styling, the Classic Flap fully embodies the spirit of the 1980s and the fashion for logos. Since its official launch in 1983, it has dethroned the brand's 2.55 flagship model and become its most sought-after bag.

CLASSIC FLAP SIZES

Extra Mini
17 × 13.5 × 8cm

Square Mini
20 × 12 × 6cm

Rectangular Mini
23 × 14.5 × 6cm

Small
25 × 14.5 × 7cm

Medium
25 × 16 × 6cm

Jumbo
30 × 20 × 9cm

Maxi Jumbo
34 × 24 × 12cm

'Diana' bag, design
by Karl Lagerf
in 1989, a variat
of the Classic Fl

ICONIC ITERATIONS

Classic Flap bag in black quilted jersey with the 'duckbill' version of the CC clasp. For jersey, the fashion house usually chose the Signature chain normally seen on the 2.55. 1983 model.

'Double Sens' Classic Flap bag in black quilted lambskin. On this model, both sides of the bag have a flap with a CC clasp. 1996 model.

'Maxi Jumbo' Classic Flap bag in black quilted glazed leather, with interwoven chain trim, fitted with the old XL clasps. Spring/Summer 1995 collection.

Classic Flap bag in black nylon featuring Choco Bar stitching. This model comes from the travel line that the fashion house created in the early 2000s and can be recognized by the nylon typical of this collection.

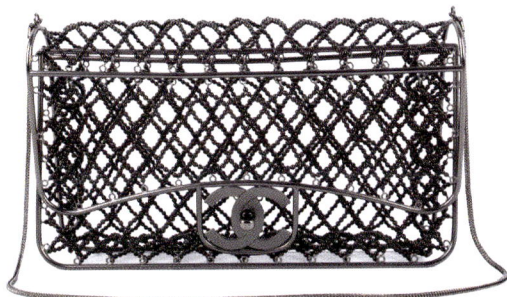

'Cage' Classic Flap bag in silver-tone beaded wire forming a quilted pattern, spirotube handle. Spring/Summer 2013 collection.

'Sand by the Sea' Classic Flap bag in transparent PVC and black lambskin with sand inserts. Spring/Summer 2019 collection.

PLU/ QUE PARFAIT

Interview with Benoît Thommeret

How did you come up with the idea of creating Plus que Parfait?

Plus que Parfait opened its doors on 11 December 2004. We specialize in selling pre-owned luxury and designer menswear. We have a selection of contemporary pieces, but also vintage and archive items. The common theme is that they are all in perfect condition.

I was one of the managers of the men's designer section at Galeries Lafayette for four years. When I left that job, I had plans to open a multi-brand designer boutique. Then I remembered all the conversations I'd had with friends and colleagues as well as the customers I met in Galeries Lafayette. They all told me they had clothes gathering dust in their wardrobes that they had rarely or never worn. I concluded from this that it would be worthwhile and innovative to open a resale store exclusively for men, offering new or like-new luxury and designer pieces. At the time, I was a pioneer!

What is the rarest piece you have ever sold?

Without hesitation, a Dior menswear sequined jacket designed by Hedi Slimane in the 2000s. It has the Union Jack on the back. A fantastic piece!

Who are your vintage icons?

Jean Paul Gaultier in first place. When I was young, I was a big fan of his first line and a keen buyer of Gaultier Junior, which unfortunately has since disappeared. I never understood why the Junior line was discontinued. Its image was so strong, and I think it should never have been stopped. And then Mugler and Montana. The 1990s, the years of my youth...everything at that time was so powerful and extravagant.

Why did you choose to work with vintage pieces?

In the beginning, I had only a few vintage pieces. Then I started looking out for them, making sure of course that they were in more than perfect condition, just like the name of my shop. Each time, it's like a little trip into the past. You realize that at a certain time it was all about the quality of the materials and the originality of the cut.

Who are your customers?

I have a very diverse clientele, both French and foreign. I try to meet every need by selecting streetwear, tailored wear, denim, casual and vintage or recent runway pieces.

What's your favourite vintage piece in your wardrobe?

It dates from the early 2000s. It's the orange Keepall by Louis Vuitton reinterpreted by Stephen Sprouse. I collect Vuitton bags, especially those made during the Virgil Abloh era. He was a great revelation for me in the world of fashion, and a master of creativity.

PLUS QUE PARFAIT
23 rue des Blancs Manteaux
75004 Paris
Instagram: @plus_que_parfait

'The 1990s,
the years of
my youth...
everything was
so powerful and
extravagant.'

Louis Vuitton Keepall bag
by Stephen Sprouse, created in 2001.

1, RUE SCRIBE.
PARIS.

Louis Vuitton

149. NEW BOND ST.

OPPOSITE CONDUIT ST

LONDON, W.

TELEGRAPHIC ADDRESS,
"VUITTON, LONDON."
TELEPHONE No 2587. GERARD.

Travelling Requisites

LOUIS VUITTON

TRAVELLING FRENCH-STYLE

Founded 170 years ago, Louis Vuitton is one of the biggest hitters in the luxury industry. Since the 19th century, innovation and travel have been powerful driving forces in the imagination of the brand. The company's founder was born into a family of modest means in 1821 in Chabouilla, a small village in the department of Jura. At the age of 14, his humdrum existence drove him to leave his native region for Paris. His journey took him to a 'box-making, packing and trunk-making' atelier in 1837, where he worked as an apprentice packing the belongings of high-society clients prior to their travels. Here he learned to make travel trunks, and his skill and know-how quickly made him the key figure in the workshop.

A REVOLUTION IN THE LUXURY INDUSTRY

The year 1852 was a defining one for Louis, who was asked to pack the belongings of Empress Eugénie. He created a complete travel set for her. Satisfied with his work, she spoke highly of it in the court, resulting in a never-ending stream of orders.

As a result, in 1854 Louis Vuitton founded his own company so that he could design luggage combining 'functionality, luxury and innovation' (the watchwords of the trunk maker). He joined forces with the English couturier Charles Frederick Worth, founder of the celebrated House of Worth, opening their first store in Paris. Both pioneers in what we now know as the 'luxury' industry, they put their signatures on their designs to protect them from counterfeiters: this was one of the first marketing operations in history.

Louis Vuitton anticipated the changes taking place at the time: the transportation boom (via locomotive, steamboat, aeroplane and automobile) allowed the wealthy classes to travel more easily and for longer. He therefore set about developing a revolutionary technique: he covered one of his trunks with coated canvas, a particularly hard-wearing material that extended the life of the trunk, was lighter than leather, and, most importantly, was completely waterproof once coated.

In 1858, he designed the basic structure of the flat, stackable trunk, which unlike the rounded trunks of the time, was more suited to all types of transport. The trunks proved so popular that Louis Vuitton had to move his workshops to Asnières-sur-Seine, connected to not only the river but the all-important railway network, as his premises in Paris had become too cramped.

VUITTON GOES INTERNATIONAL

In 1867, Louis Vuitton, at just 46 years old, was already a hugely symbolic figure in the French luxury industry, and in that year his company took part in the 1867 Paris Exposition. He was joined by his son Georges who was driven by the same passion for travel and excellence. The son encouraged his father to export their designs beyond France. Stores opened first on Oxford Street in London and then in New York and Philadelphia. The company was now of international standing.

WARDROBE

Always on the lookout for innovative ideas, Louis Vuitton listened to the wise advice of his friend Charles Frederick Worth who assured him that crinolines were likely to be abandoned in favour of less bulky garments more suitable for travel. Louis Vuitton quickly realized that he needed to design a more modern type of luggage that would be better adapted to this new attire. In 1875, he developed a new trunk designed to be opened vertically, consisting of a hanging space on one side and a set of drawers on the other, which meant that travellers did not have to unpack their personal effects upon arrival. It was known as the Wardrobe.

FAKES

Designed to prevent it being copied, the Monogram canvas has ironically become the most counterfeited fabric in the history of fashion and luxury.

A victim of his own success, Louis Vuitton's designs were widely copied. So, in 1872, to differentiate his products from his imitators, he launched a red-and-beige striped pattern to replace his Trianon grey canvas. But he did not stop there. Louis and Georges (who succeeded his father as the head of the company in 1880) launched a new, more complex print that was more difficult to imitate: a brown-and-beige checkerboard motif interjected with 'Marque L. Vuitton déposée' (L. Vuitton registered trademark) in unique lettering. When his father died in 1892, Georges took over the reins of the empire, with the same ambition and the same commitment to innovation. Once again, with the aim of differentiating Vuitton products from those of other trunk makers, he set about developing the Monogram canvas. Looking for an image that would instantly identify his products, he eventually created a pattern inspired by traditional Japanese art.

THE DRIVE FOR CONSTANT INNOVATION

The Vuitton empire continued to grow from these early foundations. Another notable concept invented by Georges was the 'unpickable' lock. Designed in 1890, it would be fitted to every trunk subsequently produced. Trunk owners were given a personal lock number and a unique key to open all their luggage.

The Cabin Trunk and Steamer Bag (used to store worn laundry on transatlantic crossings) could be slipped under a berth and revolutionized travel on luxury liners. The Driver Bag was designed for cars and could be stored inside a spare tyre; the Aero

Trunk weighed only 26kg when full, making it ideal for air travel, which became more widespread following the first powered flight in the early 20th century. The Vuitton empire entered the new century in spectacular style, given the critical role canvas appeared to have in the future of the luggage industry. During the Roaring Twenties, Louis Vuitton became a household name among wealthy families.

In 1912, Louis Vuitton built an Art Deco-inspired multi-level shop on the Champs-Élysées: this building would become the flagship store of the luxury company. It was not until 1987 and the merger with Moët Hennessy (resulting in the creation of the LVMH group) that the commitment to innovation, which had been one of the brand's strengths, would once again come to the fore. Founder of LVMH Bernard Arnault was responsible for this development when he appointed Marc Jacobs as creative director in 1997 and tasked him with creating a ready-to-wear department, which the fashion house had previously lacked.

STEPHEN SPROUSE EDITIONS

Stephen Sprouse once said: 'Rock, art and fashion were always my favourite things, in that order. But because I never learned to play an instrument, I had to focus on the other two.' Marc Jacobs first met Sprouse, an active member of the 1980s New York scene and participant in multiple forms of pop culture, in Tokyo in 1984, although it was not until 2001 that the artist began to collaborate on Vuitton designs, including the famous Graffiti logo bags.

Following Sprouse's death in 2004, Marc Jacobs decided to launch a posthumous line of accessories and clothing featuring the designs created by the American artist. The creative director revived the famous Graffiti design developed in 2001, expanding the colour palette to include green, pink and orange, and added Sprouse-inspired rose motifs to his own creations. This new commemorative line was available from January 2009.

DATE CODES

Like many luxury brands, Louis Vuitton marked its products with a date code, which it first introduced in 1982. In 2021, the fashion house replaced these numbers with microchips.

From 1982 to the mid-1980s
▶ 839 The first two digits indicate the year of production. The last digit indicates the month of production.

Mid- to late-1980s
▶ 884V.I. The first two digits indicate the year of production. The third digit indicates the month of production. The letters indicate the code of the factory where the item was made.

From early 1990 to 2006
▶ MI0989 The letters indicate the code of the factory where the item was made. The first and third digits indicate the month of production. The second and last digits indicate the year of production.

From 2004 to 2021
▶ CA2182 The letters indicate the code of the factory where the item was made. The first and third digits indicate the week of production. The second and last digits indicate the year of production.

MATERIALS

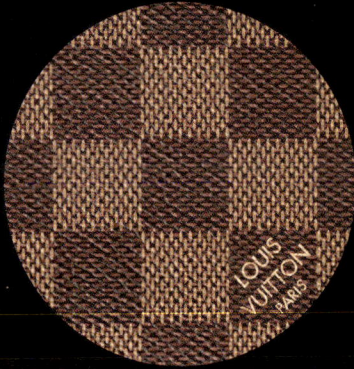

First created by Louis Vuitton in 1888, the Damier (checkerboard) canvas was discontinued for many years before being reintroduced into the brand's leather goods collections in 1996.

Variation with the launch of the Damier Azur canvas in 2006.

Variation for the brand's menswear line with the Damier Graphite canvas in 2008.

Created in 1896 by Georges Vuitton, the design is composed of Monogram Flowers surrounding the initials LV (this canvas was registered as a pattern in 1887 and as a trademark in 1895). Originally woven, it was applied via stencil until 1959, and then produced in printed coated cotton from the 1960s.

'Graffiti' Monogram canvas, launched in 2001.

Reissue of the 'Graffiti' Monogram canvas, launched in 2009.

'Denim' Monogram canvas, launched in 2005 and available in several colours.

'Idylle' Monogram canvas, launched in 2010; it replaced the line known as 'Mini Lin' and was available in several colours.

'Reverse' Monogram canvas, launched in 2016.

'Éclipse' Monogram canvas (menswear line), marketed in 2016.

The Japanese artist developed 33 colours for the creation of his Monogram canvas, produced in both black and white backdrops. It was launched in 2003.

TAKASHI MURAKAMI EDITIONS

Known as Japan's answer to Andy Warhol, Takashi Murakami mixes the manga universe with traditional culture in his designs. Marc Jacobs discovered his work in an exhibition at the Cartier Foundation in the early 2000s. 'It's not my work. No, it's a collaboration. It's not the Monogram Multicolore, it's a concept,' said the Japanese artist about this new Vuitton range.

LEATHERS

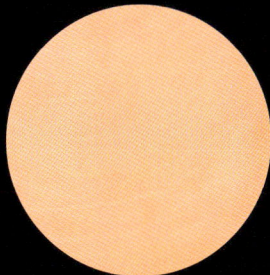

Natural leather is the signature leather of the Louis Vuitton brand. This cowhide leather is tanned using natural plant extracts, which allows the material to develop a patina over time. It is therefore important not to expose it to water, perfume or cosmetic creams. When buying a new bag, the leather will probably be very light in colour as it has not yet acquired a patina.

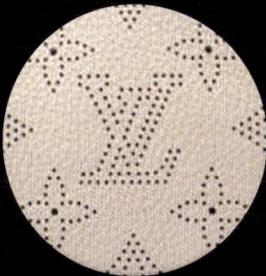

Mahina leather was launched in 2007 and is a soft perforated calfskin.

Epi leather is a reinterpretation of an older leather used by the brand and is known as Maroquin leather. It was used for luggage during the 1920s and offers good scratch resistance.

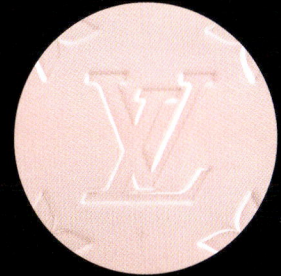

Monogram Vernis leather was introduced by Marc Jacobs in 1997. Meaning 'varnish' in French, this type of shiny leather must be treated with particular care. It should not be subjected to heat or humidity and may become sticky or discoloured over time.

LININGS

Heritage canvas

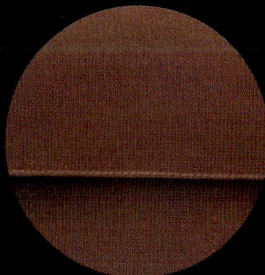

Classic canvas

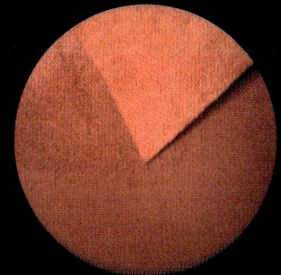

Alcantara or imitation suede

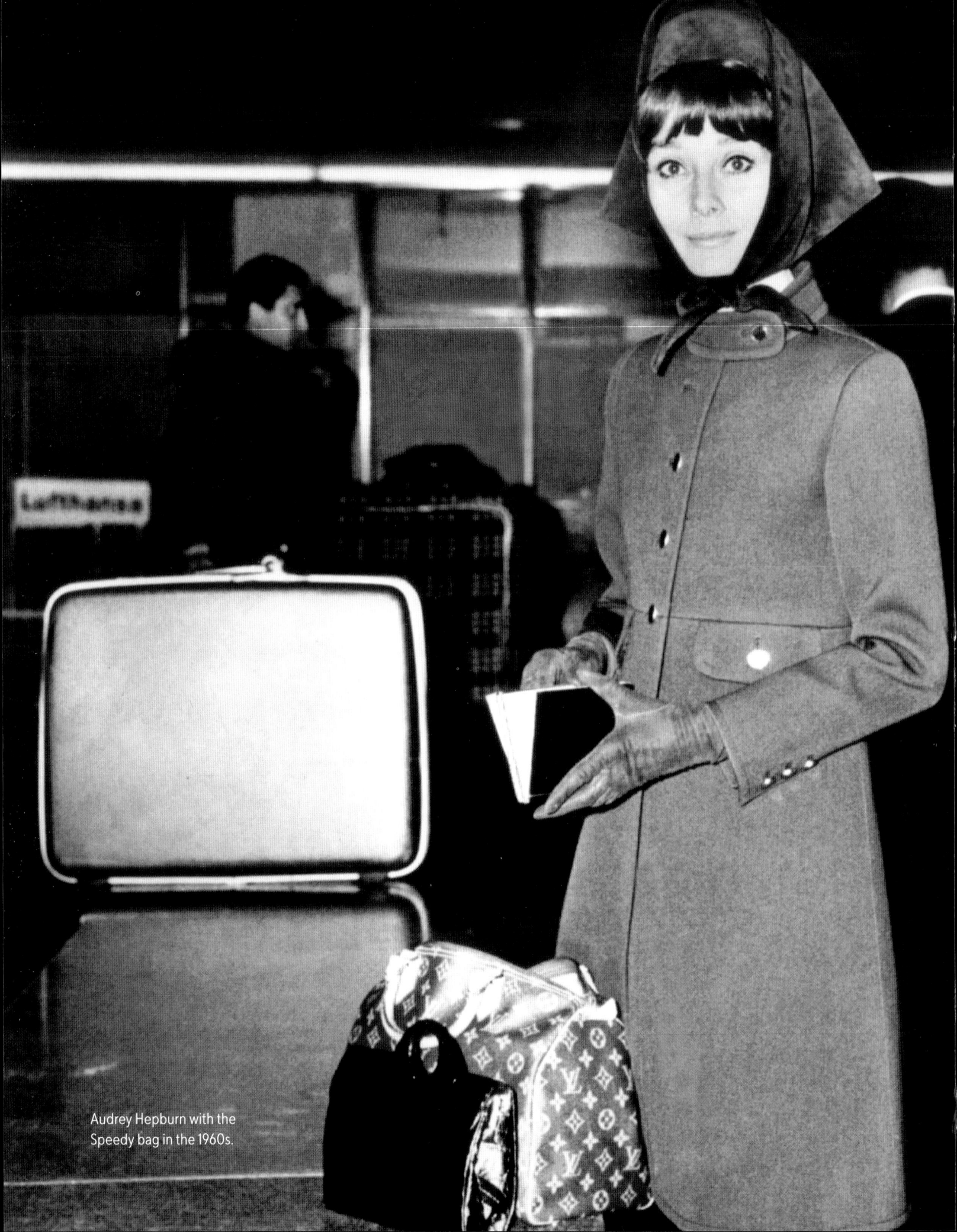

Audrey Hepburn with the
Speedy bag in the 1960s.

THE ƒPEEDY

BY LOUIƒ VUITTON

The Speedy bag is the historic model of the brand and was created in 1930. A variation of the Keepall bag, it was designed to meet demand for a city bag. Originally known as the Express, it reflected Vuitton's desire to conquer the world at high speed. It was then renamed the Speedy, a word epitomizing the boom in car use and the increasingly rapid nature of world travel.

AN ICONIC TRAVEL BAG

Originally measuring 30cm in length, like the Keepall, the Speedy had the advantage of day bags in that it could be folded and stored in a suitcase. But also like a travel bag, it came with a lock to keep belongings secure. It therefore perfectly suited the needs of city dwellers of the time and was an ideal alternative to large trunks.

As a result of its growing success, the brand decided to release the Speedy in 35 and 40cm versions. New sizes would be created later, with the Mini HL in 1978 and, more recently, the Nano Speedy and the Speedy BB. In 2011, the brand released the Speedy Bandoulière, which came with a shoulder strap (*bandoulière*) and featured two reinforced bands at either end of the bag with a D-ring at the top. This new model was produced because, although it was possible to wear other Speedy bags with a separately sold shoulder strap, attaching this to the handle rings caused the chapes to tear.

AUDREY HEPBURN, UNOFFICIAL BRAND AMBASSADOR

In the mid-1960s, Audrey Hepburn placed a special order and requested a smaller version than the original. This resulted in the release of the Speedy 25, which proved even more popular than the previous variants.

VUITTON CODES AND COLOURS

In 1997, Marc Jacobs joined Louis Vuitton as creative director and released the Speedy in a series of highly desirable limited editions. The bag was produced in striking colours or decorated with the cherries and cherry blossom of Japanese artist Takashi Murakami. Even today, no fewer than 110 processes are required to produce one bag.

In the 2000s, the famous Monogram bag was seen on the arms of all the 'It girls' of the time: Paris Hilton, Nicole Richie, Jessica Simpson and Lindsay Lohan. They all contributed to making the Speedy an iconic, must-have It bag that could be passed down the generations without losing any of its allure. With its Monogram canvas, the Speedy bag will undoubtedly stand the test of time.

'Toron' handles in natural leather

Handle ring

Leather tab

Zip pull with zip

Zip pull leather tab

Chape (*enchape*)

Piping

ICONIC ITERATIONS

Speedy bag, tribute to Stephen Sprouse, released in 2009.

Speedy bag in 'Idylle' Monogram canvas, 2010s.

Speedy bag in 'Masters' Monogram canvas, created by Jeff Koons in 2017. Wanting to mix the fashion codes of Vuitton with the world of art, the artist created a series of models based on the work of famous painters: Leonardo da Vinci, Vincent van Gogh, Peter Paul Rubens and Jean-Honoré Fragonard (shown here).

Speedy bag in gold-tone 'Miroir' Monogram canvas. This collection was inspired by the sculpture of the Keepall bag created in the 2000s by sculptor Sylvie Fleury.

Speedy bag in 'Cerise' Monogram canvas released in 2005. Takashi Murakami edition.

Neo Speedy bag in 'Denim' Monogram canvas, created in 2005.

SPEEDY SIZES

Nano Speedy
← 16cm →

Speedy BB
← 17.5cm →

Speedy 25
← 25cm →

Speedy 30
← 30cm →

Speedy 35
← 35cm →

Speedy 40
← 40cm →

Speedy bag in 'Multicolore' Monogram, produced in collaboration with Takashi Murakami.

Noé bag in Damier Azur canvas and natural leather.

THE NOÉ

BY LOUIS VUITTON

The roots of the Noé date back to the Sac à Linge *(Laundry Bag) created by* Louis Vuitton *in 1892. At the time, this bag was placed in trunks and used to store worn laundry. It was released as a standalone piece of luggage in 1927 and renamed the* Sac Marin *(Navy Bag) as it was designed for ocean liner travel. It was not until 1932 that the first version of the bag known as the Noé was produced.*

A BAG FOR CHAMPAGNE

In 1932, a champagne producer asked the House of Vuitton to design a sturdy bag to transport bottles of its precious elixir. The model had to allow its customers to carry five bottles: four the right way up, and one in the middle upside down. The bag also needed to be suitable for picnics and fit perfectly in the trunks of convertibles.

In 1958, the smaller Petit Noé was released, adopting the style now seen today, and designed as a city bag. While the original version of the bag was made entirely from natural leather to guarantee the sturdiness required, this new iteration was available in the famous Monogram canvas. From this period onwards, the bucket bag was used by women to hold all their daily essentials.

ICONIC ITERATIONS

Over the course of the bag's history, the handle was lengthened to make it more comfortable to carry on the shoulder. The arrival of the Epi leather version in the 1980s meant that customers could now choose from numerous combinations of colours and shapes. A constantly evolving bag, the brand launched the NéoNoé in 2017. The interior was divided by the addition of a central zipped pocket, and the bag fitted with a detachable handle so that it could be carried by hand (first on the all-leather versions and then on the canvas models). For over 60 years, the Noé bag has remained as sought after as ever, and its popularity continues to rise.

A BIBLICAL NAME

Noé is the French name for Noah, the biblical patriarch who saved the animals from the Great Flood. He is also said to have planted a vine on Mount Ararat. The name was therefore an obvious choice when Gaston-Louis Vuitton was thinking of what to call his bubbly-carrying bag.

Drawstring

Eyelet

Adjustable handle for shoulder wear

Half-round D-ring

Dyed edge

Reinforcement band

Square bottom

NOÉ SIZES

Nano Noé

13cm

Noé BB

22cm

Petit Noé

27cm

Grand Noé

27.5cm

Grand Noé bag in red, blue and green
Epi leather, created in 1995.

THE KEEPALL

BY LOUIS VUITTON

Now offered mainly in the brand's menswear collections, the Keepall was originally designed for Louis Vuitton's female customers. Seen today as a unisex bag, the model has continued to delight since its creation in the first half of the 20th century.

A TRAVEL BAG FOR WOMEN

Created in 1930 by Gaston-Louis Vuitton, the Keepall is a quintessential travel bag. Considered the 'big brother' of the Speedy, its origins date back to a model that the brand offered in 1892 known as the *Sac de Nuit* (Overnight Bag). This allowed women to keep their belongings nearby at a time when high society usually travelled with rigid luggage to which they had no access.

In the 1920s, always at the cutting edge of fashion, the luxury goods maker could see the growing popularity of short trips away, in the form of touring, visits to seaside resorts and cruises. The company therefore decided to design a practical and lightweight bag that would give women the freedom to travel on their own.

MODELS FOR MEN AND WOMEN

The first version of the Keepall was made from cotton canvas. It was not until the 1960s that Monogram canvas was used for this model. The classic design quickly won over male customers with its modern lines.

In the 1980s, a version with a shoulder strap was released and featured reinforcements on the sides so that it could be worn on the shoulder or crossbody. When first created, the Keepall was available in four classic sizes: 45, 50, 55 and 60cm; there are now also smaller versions such as the Keepall XS (25cm) and the City Keepall (27cm), with the latter being worn only over the shoulder as it has no handles.

Louis Vuitton City Keepall bag in 'Eclipse' Monogram canvas, 2023.

'Toron' handles in natural leather

Hard zip pulls and zip

Handle ring

Leather tab

Side bands

Piping

KEEPALL SIZES

Keepall 45
45 × 27 × 20cm

Keepall 50
50.04 × 28.96 × 22.10cm

Keepall 55
55 × 31 × 24cm

Keepall 60
60 × 33 × 26cm

ICONIC ITERATIONS

Almost every year, the creative directors at the helm of Louis Vuitton offer limited editions and variations of the Keepall, in line with its status as the brand's best-seller.

Keepall bag in Graffiti Monogram canvas, produced under the creative direction of Marc Jacobs. Stephen Sprouse edition, 2001.

Backpack Keepall bag in Cobalt Damier canvas, produced under the creative direction of Kim Jones, 2014.

Keepall XS bag in Taurillon leather and 'Distorted' Damier canvas, under the creative direction of Virgil Abloh. Spring/Summer 2021 collection.

'Van Gogh' Keepall Bandoulière bag. 'Masters' Monogram edition by Jeff Koons, 2017.

'Architettura' Keepall Bandoulière bag created in collaboration with luxury brand Fornasetti. Capsule Collection, 2021.

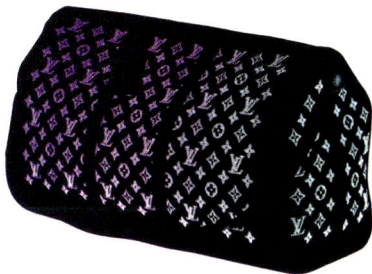

'LED' Keepall Bandoulière bag produced under the creative direction of Virgil Abloh. Autumn/Winter 2019 menswear collection. A technical design feat, the bag is made from a jacquard weave of Light-Up optic fibres to create the Monogram motif, with the wearer able to choose how the fibres change colour.

'Prism' Keepall Bandoulière bag produced under the creative direction of designer Virgil Abloh. Spring/Summer 2019 menswear collection.

THE ALMA

BY LOUIS VUITTON

The foundations of the Alma bag were laid in 1934 with the creation of a model called the Squire. Gaston Louis Vuitton, the founder's grandson, designed this highly structured and rigid bag with a square base and rounded upper corners in Art Deco style. It takes its name from place de l'Alma, which connects two stylish districts in Paris. In 1955, a new version was designed known as the Champs Élysées. The body of the bag was placed on a reinforced base, bringing it a step closer to the current Alma model.

PARISIAN LUXURY

The lines of the bag inspired by the Art Deco era are still visible today on the modern model released in 1992 and known as the Alma. It takes its name from the square connecting avenue Montaigne and the Champs-Élysées.

ALMA BRANCHES OUT

The Alma bag took over from the Speedy and became the brand's second-biggest-selling handbag. With a rigid structure, it retains its shape and cannot be folded into a suitcase. It comes in seven sizes: the Nano Alma, Alma BB, Alma PM, Alma MM, Alma GM and the Alma Travel in two different sizes (45 and 50cm along the length of the base). In 2010, the BB version of the bag was released with a detachable and adjustable shoulder strap for a new generation of customers.

A BAG FOR GABRIELLE

The first version of the Alma bag is said to have been a special order produced for the couturière Gabrielle Chanel.

e Alma bag in 'Multicolore' Monogram
nvas. Takashi Murakami edition.

'The name Louis Vuitton is a magical word that makes me travel, even when sitting at my work table.'
Azzedine Alaïa

'Toron' handles

Leather tie (*tige*)

Handle rings, some fitted with shoulder strap attachment

Riveted chapes (*enchapes*)

Dyed edge

Bell lanyard (*clochette*)

Zip pulls with zip

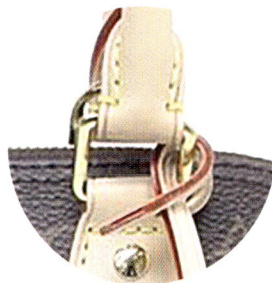

Dyed edge

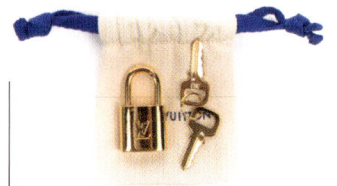

Lock

ALMA SIZES

Nano Alma
16.5 × 13 × 8cm

Alma BB
23.5 × 17.5 × 11.5cm

Alma PM
32 × 25 × 16cm

Alma MM
36 × 28 × 17cm

Alma GM
38 × 28 × 18cm

ICONIC ITERATIONS

Alma bag in 'Multicolore' Monogram canvas on white backdrop with natural leather (31 × 24 × 17cm), created in 2004. Takashi Murakami edition.

'Multicolore' Monogram

Riveted chapes (*enchapes*)

Long Alma bag in white glazed leather with nude graffiti motif. Stephen Sprouse edition, 2001.

Long Alma bag in cerise 'Mini Lin' Monogram canvas, 2001.

Nano Alma bag in black Monogram lurex satin, 2010.

Alma bag in Monogram canvas and leopard-print calfskin
Louis Vuitton × Azzedine Alaïa, 1996. To mark the centenary of the Monogram canvas, Louis Vuitton asked seven giants from the world of fashion and art to design new variations of the bag. Azzedine Alaïa, Manolo Blahnik, Roméo Gigli, Helmut Lang, Isaac Mizrahi, Sybilla and Vivienne Westwood were the lucky designers chosen for this collaboration. Each of their creations embodied their distinctive style while preserving the identity of the famous canvas.

Alaïa's collaboration with Vuitton allowed him to express his talents as a visual artist, his love of glamour, and his modern and visionary outlook. The bag he created was extremely feminine, sensually tied in pony hair leather printed with a leopard motif, and also included cases and pouches of all sizes for different types of cosmetics.

Alma BB bag in yellow Epi leather with black Infinity Dots print, 2023, created with Japanese artist Yayoi Kusama.

THE PAPILLON

BY LOUIS VUITTON

The Papillon bag was created by the brand in 1966. Like the Speedy, it shares some features of the Keepall. However, the fashion house mostly drew its inspiration from the street and the latest trends, which were perfectly embodied by model and fashion icon Twiggy.

A BAG FOR EVERYDAY USE

After a stroll along the Champs-Élysées, Henry-Louis Vuitton was moved to design a bag with two thin leather handles evoking the delicate wings of a butterfly (*papillon* in French). The choice of name for the bag was therefore obvious.

The following year, in 1967, *Vogue* immortalized the famous model Twiggy carrying the bag in her hand, and an icon was born.

A HERITAGE PIECE IN MULTIPLE VARIATIONS

Like many of the brand's designs, numerous iterations of the Papillon have been produced. Originally made in brown grained leather, it was not until 2002 that the handles appeared in natural leather. In the 1990s, a version of the Papillon was created in Epi leather known as the 'Sufflot'. In the early 2000s, another iteration, the 'Bedford', was made from Monogram Vernis leather.

In 2022, the brand released a new version reinterpreted by Nicolas Ghesquière: the rigid Papillon 'Trunk' replicates both the heritage of the Papillon bag and the hallmarks of the legendary Vuitton trunks.

The Papillon 'Trunk' bag in Monogram canvas, created in 2022.

TRIBUTE TO THE PAPILLON

Using the Papillon model for inspiration, in 2006 Japanese architect Shigeru Ban, in association with Jean de Gastines, installed a temporary dome structure on the roof terrace of the Louis Vuitton buildings at the corner of avenue Georges V in Paris. The dome was supported by cardboard tubes wrapped in Louis Vuitton canvas, and the whole structure was covered with a white canvas. The details of the construction were borrowed from the vocabulary of leather goods; for example, the braced frame of the structure was made from leather in the style of the handles on a Papillon bag.

Dyed edge

Mid-length handles in natural leather

Zip closure

Zip pull leather tab

Zip pull

Handle ring

Lock

Side bands

Piping

Gold snap clasp with stamp ('Trunk').

Louis Vuitton monogram on the chain ('Trunk').

S-lock closure with stamp ('Trunk').

Papillon bag in Monogram canvas and natural leather, with its interior zipped pouch.

ICONIC ITERATIONS

Papillon bag in 'Cherry Blossom' Monogram canvas, Takashi Murakami edition, created in 2003.

Papillon bag in Damier Ebène canvas, created in 2004.

Papillon 'Bedford' bag in orange Monogram Vernis leather, 2004.

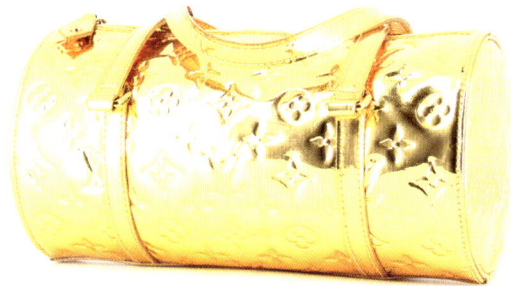

Papillon bag in 'Miroir Monogram', created in 2006.

Papillon 'Soufflot' bag in black Epi leather, created in 1997.

Papillon 'Trunk' bag in Monogram canvas and cocoa leather reminiscent of the Lozine leather trim on the brand's luggage. Its dimensions are extremely precise: 19 × 9 × 9cm.

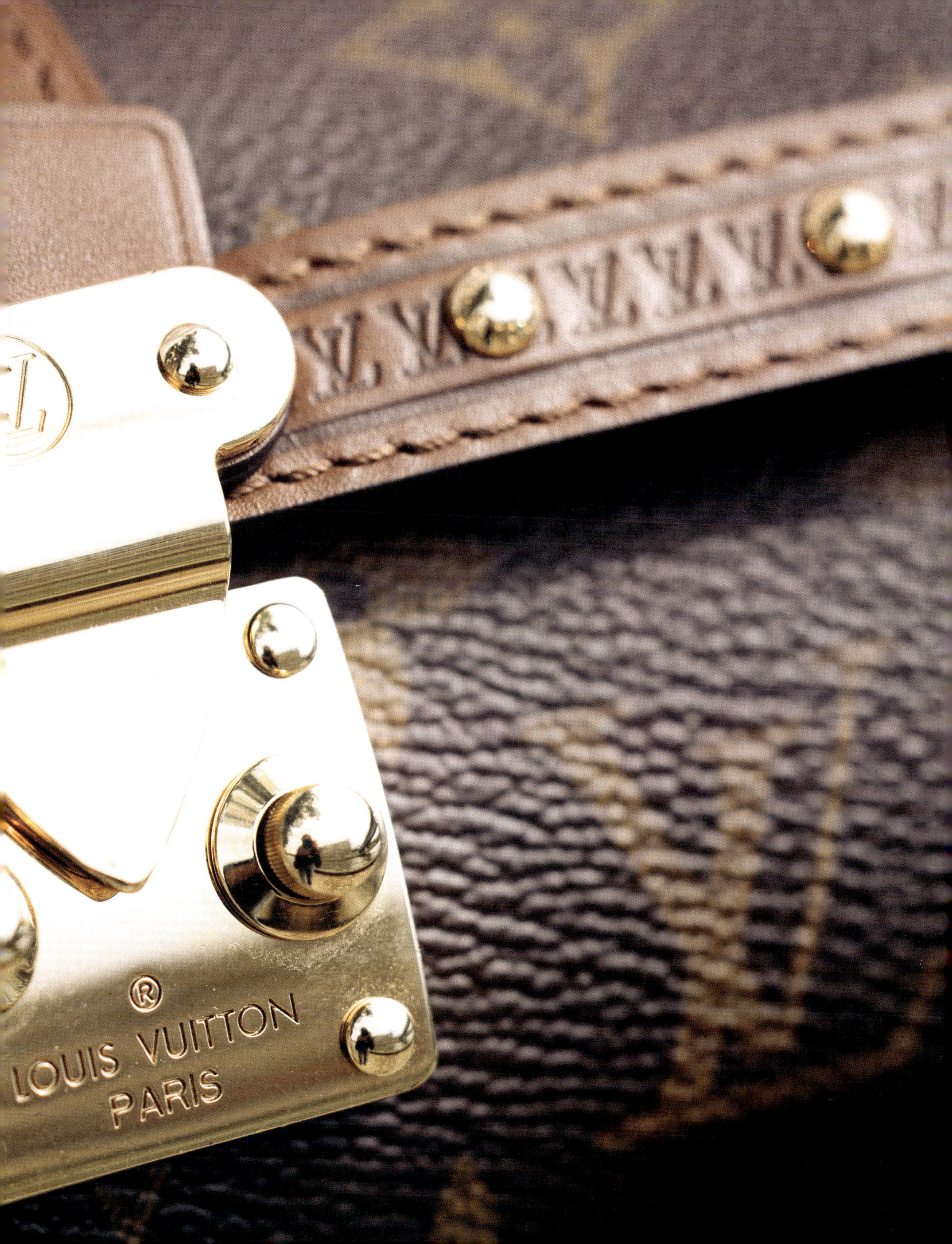
®
LOUIS VUITTON
PARIS

THE SAC PLAT

BY LOUIS VUITTON

The name Sac Plat, or Flat Bag, was used twice by Louis Vuitton for two different designs that shared the common feature of a slender profile when flattened. The earlier version could be easily stored in a trunk and was perfect for an overnight stay.

A 'REVOLUTIONARY' BAG

The model we are familiar with today was released at a momentous time in history: the year 1968. The bag, too, quickly became 'revolutionary'. The events of May 1968 in France and Europe contributed to the emancipation of women and the emergence of a new approach to gender equality. This bag was a perfect response and would become one of the trump cards of the invincible businesswomen of the 1970s and 1980s: it was easy to handle, easy to get into, and suitable for both work and leisure activities. Louis Vuitton successfully identified the trend of the moment, ensuring the brand was in total synchronicity with societal developments.

STYLES AND VARIATIONS

Available in two sizes, it was appreciated for its simplicity: a Monogram canvas body with two handles in natural leather. Less widely available between 2000 and 2010, a few years ago Louis Vuitton released a scaled-down and modernized version of the Sac Plat that can be worn crossbody. The 'Venice' bag is a variant, coming in the same shape as the Sac Plat but with a zip closure for greater security.

'Toron' handles

Dyed edge

Handle ring

Rivet

Riveted chapes (*enchapes*)

Gusset

AN ICONIC VARIANT

The love story between Louis Vuitton and Japan was originally brought to life in the early 2000s through the designs of Takashi Murakami, a major figure in contemporary art and manga culture. In 2005, Marc Jacobs once again collaborated with the artist to develop a line of bags in 'Cerise' Monogram canvas screen-printed with cherry (*cerise*) motifs. With a fresh feel, the line offered five new urban models and was available on some of the brand's iconic pieces.

The new line featured red stitching and red lining. The pattern added a sense of fun and light-heartedness to the bag thanks to the different expressions of the cherries: whether surprised, smiling or bewildered, they brightened up a collection that had a relatively serious reputation.

Red lining and stitching.
The cherries have very different expressions,
from astonishment to intense happiness.

THE BAMBOO

BY GUCCI

How did bamboo, an exotic material grown in climes far removed from Italy, become the signature product of Gucci? In the post war period, faced with a shortage of leather and significant restrictions on importing it, Guccio Gucci had to source new, easy-to-find materials in order to continue producing bags. In 1947, he came up with the idea of using bamboo cane, a material originating in Japan that was not subject to import restrictions, and therefore easy to bring into Italy for making his pieces.

MANUFACTURING TECHNIQUES

Bamboo is used for the handle and clasp of the bag. Bending bamboo cane is no easy task: it has to be soaked in water and subjected to heat to give the cane the desired shape. Once this is obtained, several layers of varnish are applied to protect the bamboo and give it a shiny appearance.

A MUST-HAVE MATERIAL

The Bamboo bag – its original workshop name was the 0633 bag – quickly became a must-have piece worn by Hollywood stars. It continues to be a flagship item in the catalogue of the Florentine fashion house and is available in several colours, sizes and leathers. Bamboo has become a signature material for Gucci, and the brand also uses it in the production of other models such as the roomy Diana tote bag, which features a bamboo handle, and the Indy bag, with bamboo details.

A PATENTED IDEA

In the 1950s, Gucci filed a patent for the use of bamboo in bags to prevent other fashion houses from copying the idea.

ICONIC ITERATIONS

Gucci backpacks in velvet with bamboo handle and clasp.

Bullet bag in leather with bamboo details.

Half Moon bag with bamboo handle.

Indy bag with bamboo details.

Bamboo proved so popular with the public that Gucci used the material to produce other flagship products.

Gucci bangle in solid silver replicating a bamboo cane.

Gucci key ring in gold-tone metal and bamboo.

Gucci necklace in silver and bamboo.

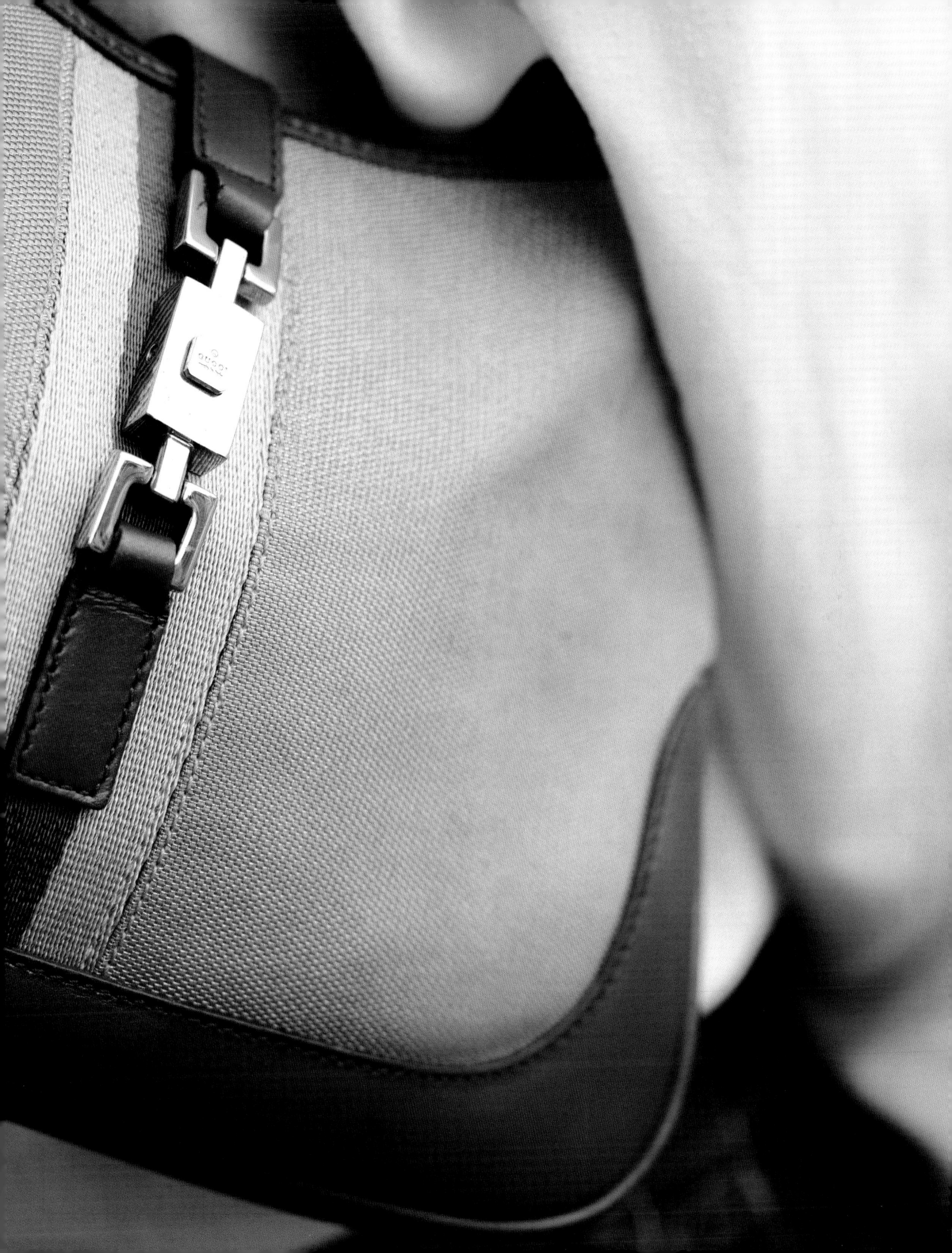

THE JACKIE

BY GUCCI

Like many other luxury bags, this iconic piece from the House of Gucci owes its name to a woman – in this instance, a woman as iconic in the world of fashion as she was on the international political and socialite scene. The First Lady of the United States would later become the wife of Aristotle Onassis, who in the 1960s was one of the richest men in the world. Yes, the Gucci Jackie bag was named after none other than Jacqueline Kennedy, a woman of influence who gave the model its immortal status.

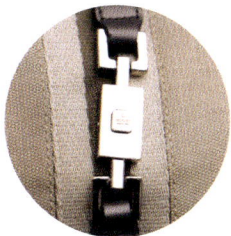

The Jackie features different types of closures such as the hook clasp (top), which is widely used today, and the piston clasp (bottom) with the Gucci stamp.

JACKIE'S BAG

Created in 1961 by Gucci, the Jackie features casual styling and was originally called the Fifties Constance. With a half-moon shape and short handle for wearing on the shoulder and large enough to be worn during the day, it was quickly spotted by Jacqueline Kennedy, a big fan of this type of bag. She was often photographed with slouchy bags on her shoulder. But it was Gucci who paid the highest tribute to this lady by giving her name to the bag: in 1964, the model was renamed the Jackie in honour of its ambassador. From the streets of Manhattan to the coves of Capri, she was regularly photographed with the bag attached to her shoulder. The story even goes that the relatively large size of the bag allowed her to protect herself from unwelcome paparazzi.

A MUCH-REVISITED BAG

The Jackie was a Gucci best-seller for many years. After falling out of favour at the beginning of the 1990s, it was returned to the limelight by Tom Ford who reinterpreted it to create a less austere look. The bag has continued to change through the decades: the clasp has been modernized, the handle has varied in length, and the option of adding a shoulder strap has been introduced.

ICONIC ITERATIONS

Jackie bag in suede with lobster clasp
The handle is in bamboo, a material widely used by Gucci.

Two Jackie bags in monogram canvas with different types of clasp.

Jackie bag in canvas and leather with floral print
A modern reinterpretation of the 'Flora' print.

KELLY AND JACKIE
Created in 1966 by Vittorio Accornero for Gucci, the iconic Gucci 'Flora' print was originally designed for a scarf gifted to Grace Kelly.

'Quality is remembered long after price is forgotten.'
Gucci

Jackie Kennedy in Manhattan, New York, in the 1970s, wearing the iconic Gucci bag.

THE LADY DIOR

BY CHRISTIAN DIOR

The Lady Dior bag is the iconic leather goods piece from the House of Dior – a timeless classic that entered the pantheon of legendary bags at lightning speed.

A BAG FOR DIANA

In September 1995, a major exhibition on French Post-Impressionist painter Paul Cézanne was held at the Grand Palais in Paris. The French presidential couple, Jacques and Bernadette Chirac, wanted to offer a gift to Princess Diana who was attending the event. So they asked the House of Dior to design an exclusive piece. The new bag was unveiled at the exhibition prior to its official release.

It was designed by Gianfranco Ferré, the creative director at the time. He produced a model with a cannage motif reminiscent of the cane-backed Napoleon III chairs on which Christian Dior seated spectators at his couture shows. Ever faithful to the identity of the founder, Gianfranco Ferré placed metal letters (D, I, O, R) on one of the handles in the style of lucky charms, as a way of paying homage to the talismans beloved by the couturier.

FROM THE 'CHOUCHOU' TO THE LADY

The bag, unofficially known as the 'Chouchou' (a French term of endearment), made its first appearance at the 1995 runway show held at the Musée d'Art Moderne de la Ville de Paris. Diana's love of the piece made it an immediate success. The Princess of Wales became the ambassador for the bag, which was briefly renamed the Princesse. Now firmly established as an It bag, in 1996 it adopted its definitive name with Diana's agreement: it would be known as the Lady Dior.

FASHION ICON

The model proved so popular that just two years after its release, 200,000 models had already been sold.

*'The couturier knows it:
every woman is a princess.'*

Christian Dior

Square shape

Gold-tone or silver-tone
metal charms

Quilted, topstitched finish
with cannage motif

LADY DIOR SIZES

| **Micro** | **Mini** | **Small** | **Medium** | **Large** |
| ← 15cm → | ← 17cm → | ← 20cm → | ← 24cm → | ← 32cm → |

ICONIC ITERATIONS

1998 Lady Dior in satin with 'rhinestones' forming the cannage motif.

Lady Dior in black lambskin with cannage stitching.

Lady Dior in purple python and crystals, Spring/Summer 2010 collection.

Lady Dior in multi-coloured glossy astrakhan and silver-tone metal, 2014.

Lady Dior in openwork multi-coloured python, Spring/Summer 2014 collection.

Lady Dior in painted silk and black leather. In 2016, the fashion house launched 'Lady Dior Art', asking artists from around the world to reinterpret the famous model each year.

Lady Dior in multi-coloured leather with beads, 2017.

Lady Dior in black leather with multi-coloured beads, 'Resort' collection 2019.

Lady Dior in black-and-white houndstooth canvas, 2022 collection. An iconic motif of the fashion house in the 1950s.

As the founder of ALE PARIS, how would you define yourself and why this name?

I define myself as a couturier and a craftsman, and as a fan of vintage luxury clothing. I like fabrics, materials and the construction of clothing; I love analysing the details of how a jacket or dress is put together – for me there's a form of perfection in a Chanel or Yves Saint Laurent jacket. As for the name, it's a shortened form of my first name, and the logo is the phonetic transcription of how my mother pronounces it!

How did you set up ALE PARIS?

I've always been interested in fashion and designers from the 1980s and 1990s. After studying translation and interpreting in Madrid, I knew it wasn't for me, so I decided to follow my passion and studied fashion design and modelling at a Parisian fashion school. Once I had my qualifications, I worked for designers in Paris, but I'm very independent, so in 2018 I decided to open my own boutique selling both personal designs and vintage luxury clothing and accessories. I was lucky enough to find a really beautiful space over two floors in the passage du Grand-Cerf, a listed arcade that's delightfully charming.

'In terms of vintage luxury, you will only find pieces that I love sourced from the 1970s, 1980s, 1990s and 2000s.'

What do you offer in your store?

I have my own on-site workshop in the basement; I don't create collections but I sell ready-to-wear pieces for men and women and also offer a bespoke design service. In terms of vintage luxury, you will only find pieces that I love sourced from the 1970s, 1980s, 1990s and 2000s, and that can be easily worn by today's women.

Which brands or designers do you particularly like?

I adore Yves Saint Laurent, and a whole rack in the store is entirely dedicated to the brand. I also collect the costume jewellery that Roger Scemama and Robert Goossens created for YSL, Christian Lacroix and Chanel: it's almost become an addiction! I love the designs of Thierry Mugler, Galliano for Dior and Margaretha Ley for Escada, for example. Of course, I can also fall for other brands and designers.

For my selection of bags, I intuitively go for what feels right: Gucci, Fendi, Celine, Loewe, Vuitton and Chanel. When a bag is already being worn by too many people on the street, it's time to move on. Fashion should allow you to stand out from the crowd!

What do customers like about coming to your store?

I develop a very personal relationship with customers who share my passion for vintage clothing and appreciate how I select my pieces. Over time, I get to know the measurements and tastes of my loyal customers: I'm like their personal shopper and I work hard to find *the* piece that's missing from their collection. My Parisian, American and Asian customers are all luxury enthusiasts, and we understand each other well.

ALE PARIS
6 passage du Grand-Cerf
75002 Paris
Instagram: @aleparisboutique
www.aleparis.fr

Christian Dior Saddle bag, Autumn/ Winter 2000 collection, designed by John Galliano. 'Dior Newspaper Gazette' print on leather. This model is one of the most sought-after versions.

THE SADDLE

BY CHRISTIAN DIOR

The Saddle is a rare species in the world of leather goods: one of the few It bags that is now back in fashion years after it was first released in 1999. It owes its fame to the many personalities who have worn it, from Paris Hilton to Sarah Jessica Parker in the iconic series Sex and the City.

'Real elegance is everywhere. Especially in the things that don't show.' Christian Dior

THE IT BAG OF THE 2000s

Designed in 1999 for the Spring/Summer 2000 runway show, the Saddle was the work of John Galliano, the creative director of the fashion house at the time. Originally called the Logo bag, it was renamed the Saddle two years later in recognition of its distinctive shape. The model rode the fashion wave for bags worn on the shoulder and highly distinctive logos. It quickly became a worldwide success.

RETURN TO GRACE

However, like all It bags, its decline was rapid. Following the difficult departure of John Galliano and the numerous aesthetic changes of the period, Dior discontinued production of the Saddle. Forgotten for years, it resurfaced in 2014 when Beyoncé was seen with a model on her arm. But it is mostly thanks to Maria Grazia Chiuri, creative director of the fashion house since 2018, that we owe the resurrection of the legendary bag. For her first Autumn/Winter runway show, the designer included the unexpected return of the Saddle, this time featuring smooth leathers and embroidery. Whether vintage or recent models, fans fought to get their hands on a bag that had been shunned for many years.

FLUCTUATING PRICES

Because the Saddle had been neglected by customers for years, in the 2010s it was possible to buy pre-owned models at bargain prices. In 2018, however, the price of vintage models started to rocket on the pre-loved market. In the world of fashion, what goes around comes around.

Mini Saddle in black satin
with 'rhinestone' metal
elements, 2001.

ICONIC ITERATIONS

Saddle in kid, Autumn/Winter 2000 collection.

Saddle in Dior Oblique canvas, 2001.

Saddle in camouflage printed canvas, 2001.

Saddle in Dior Oblique canvas with multi-coloured floral motif, Spring/Summer 2001.

Saddle in patchwork printed canvas, 2003.

Saddle in leather with leopard print, 2003.

THE BAGUETTE

BY FENDI

An It bag with French credentials, this piece was designed by Italian brand Fendi and released in 1997. It was quickly popularized by Carrie Bradshaw, the fashionista protagonist of cult series Sex and the City.

A PICTURE-POSTCARD IMAGE

The name 'Baguette' was the invention of its designer, Silvia Venturini Fendi (grand-daughter of the brand's founders, Adele and Edoardo Fendi): she created the bag to be slipped under the arm, in homage to the picture-postcard image of Parisians carrying their freshly baked baguettes. The flap of the Baguette bag is closed with a stylized clasp made up of two interlocking Fs, replicating the logo of the fashion house. The bag has an interior zipped pocket and can be carried on the shoulder using a short handle.

AN ICONIC CLASP

The success of the bag was probably due to the clasp displaying the interlocking Fs of Fendi. In the early 2000s, 'logomania' reached dizzying heights and brand logos were exhibited in striking and intentional ways, becoming the kings of the fashion world.

'FUN FUR'

The Fendi logo, with its double F, also known as the Zucca, was created by Karl Lagerfeld in 1965. Rather than referring to the brand, the two Fs are in fact an acronym for the expression 'Fun Fur', which was created by the designer to describe his vision for that luxurious material. Originally, the logo was used only on luggage and in the linings of fur coats.

ICONIC ITERATIONS

While the Baguette bag was originally designed to be carried only under
the arm, current models have a long detachable shoulder strap for crossbody
wear. Another wider and taller version with more capacity and better suited to
everyday needs was also created under the name Mamma Baguette. Around
a hundred variations of the bag exist in different sizes, colours and materials.

Mamma Baguette Fendi bag.

Selleria Baguette in leather,
decorated with the large Selleria
stitching typical of Fendi.

Baguette, in collaboration with fashion house Porter, sold with three interchangeable shoulder straps. Spring/Summer 2019 menswear collection.

Baguette in black nylon and silver-tone hardware.

Baguette in purple suede.

LUXURY & PRIM

How did you come up with the idea of creating Luxury & Prim?

It all started in 2020 during the first lockdown: the need but, above all, the desire to do something together that reflected who we are and what we're passionate about. The obvious answer was luxury goods. With my passion for leather bags and Florian's love of watchmaking, the project was born. So we opened our own store, with an associated e-shop. Four years after opening, the team has grown and there are now three of us: me (Ameline), Florian and Jean-Luc (our store manager).

As soon as we started the project, we began to think about the type of image we wanted to create. We decided to use the services of an artist to create a space that reflects who we are: quirky, certainly, but also warm. We chose a local artist called Pleks to decorate the walls of the store. Firstly, to assert our visual identity, and secondly, to convey the many shared values that motivate us, such as animal welfare and street art.

What is your favourite piece?

It's the Chanel Boy bag from the 'Paris-Dallas' Métiers d'Art Pre-Autumn 2014 collection, which has even more of a rock vibe than the basic model.

What is the rarest piece you have ever sold?

Pieces aren't so much rare as hard to find. We've had minaudières by Chanel on a few occasions, each one more incredible than the last. My favourite is the one in Lucite and Swarovski crystals from the Autumn/Winter 2017 collection, Astronautes.

Who are your vintage icons?

Coco Chanel without a doubt...I've been mad about tweed since my teens. As I grew up, I became familiar with her background and her modern ideas; her sense of aesthetics always impressed me. Karl Lagerfeld was so good at reinterpreting the fashion codes she had already established that I couldn't help but love his work. The House of Chanel has a very special place in my heart, and my wardrobe, of course.

Why did you choose to work with vintage pieces?

Vintage isn't our core business. In fact, we prefer to work with pieces dating from at least the early 2000s, which speak to us much more. However, when it comes to timeless and iconic pieces, it's the quality and finishes of certain models that leave us in awe of all things vintage. What could be more beautiful than a vintage box calf Kelly bag in very good condition with its gold-plated fasteners and clasp? Or a lambskin Classic Flap bag from the mid-1990s? Eco-responsible consumption is also increasingly important in our lives, and we strongly believe in the beneficial impact of the pre-loved market.

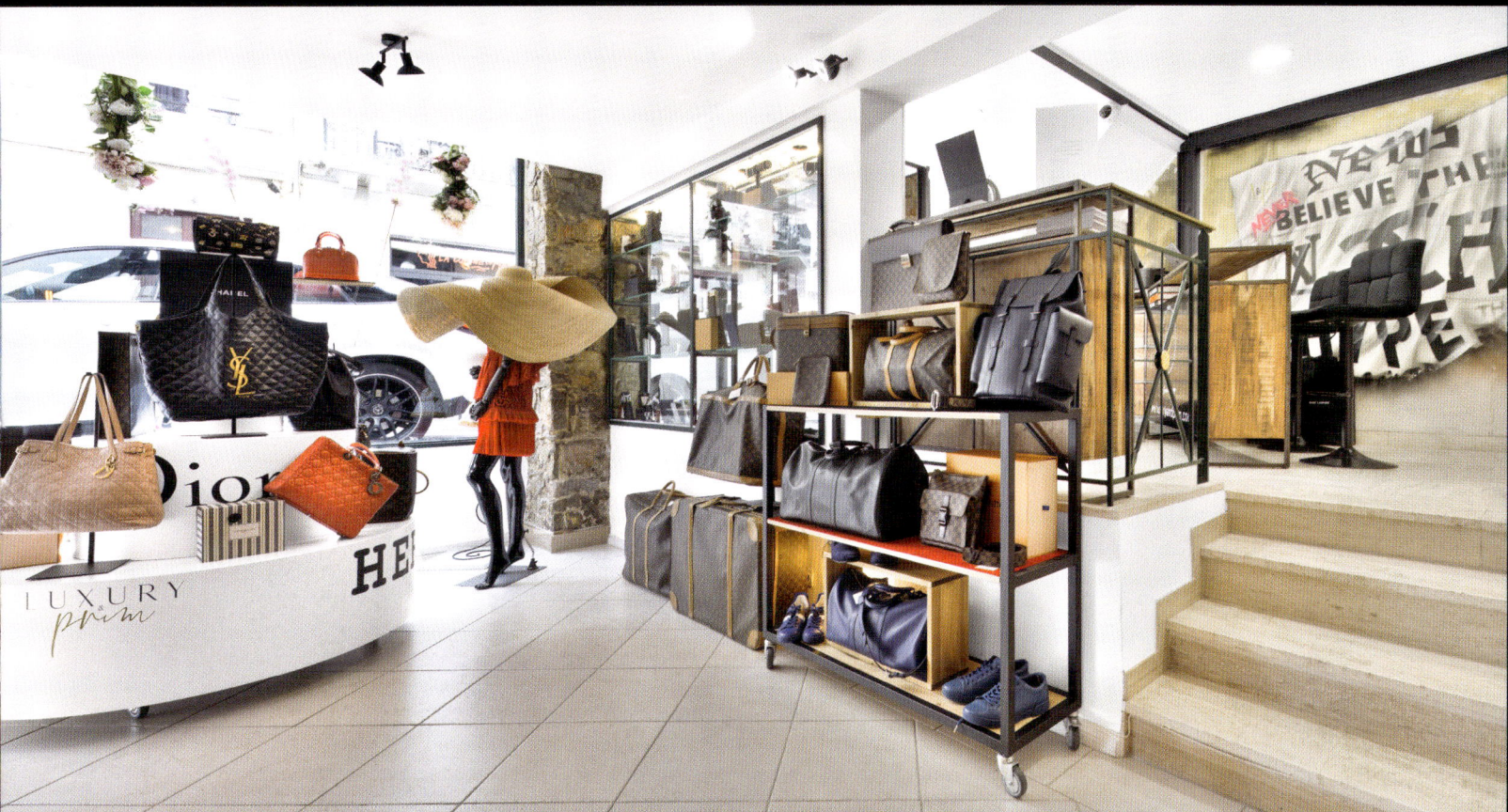

'I've been mad about tweed since my teens.'

What is the 'plus point' of your store?

Faced with rampant counterfeiting and the rise of 'super fakes' that perfectly imitate luxury brands, we decided to be the first consignment store in France to have all of our pieces appraised and authenticated by an independent expert (Louis d'Oisemont Consulting) before putting them on sale. This is reassurance for our customers that they are not buying fakes.

Do you have a typical customer profile?

We are fortunate to have loyal customers who are both local and foreign. The many events held each month in Cannes (such as the real estate show, Cannes Film Festival and Canneseries TV Festival) mean we regularly get to see clients from the four corners of the globe. After all, what could be nicer at the end of a lovely sunny day than coming to treat yourself at the store? So we don't really have typical customers as such.

LUXURY & PRIM
9 rue d'Alger
06400 Cannes
www.luxuryandprim.com

THE CHANEL JACKET

BY CHANEL

The Chanel jacket as we know it today was first produced in 1954. Its foundations, however, date back to the 1920s. At that time, Gabrielle Chanel was in a relationship with the 2nd Duke of Westminster, and his outfits were a huge source of inspiration to her.

THE INVENTION OF THE CHANEL SUIT

Gabrielle Chanel regularly borrowed the duke's clothes, which she cut up and adapted before heading out to the racecourse. The designer was already embracing a completely new take on modernity and was way ahead of what her contemporaries expected from fashion. She started to work with both jersey, a material used only for men's underwear at the time, and tweed, which was also reserved exclusively for men. However, it was not until after the Second World War that she gave the world what is undoubtedly the most recognizable couture piece of all time: the Chanel suit.

A DISRUPTIVE DESIGN

Chanel's return to France in 1953 was hardly propitious: her connections with certain Nazi dignitaries and her outspoken attitudes made her re-entry on to the creative scene problematic. Europe shunned her first collection, but in the United States her Chanel designs were instantly snapped up. To make matters worse, Gabrielle adopted a stance that was out of step with the times, believing that Christian Dior's New Look once again imprisoned women in their clothes: 'I, who love women, wanted to give her clothes in which she would be comfortable, in which she could drive a car, yet at the same time clothes which emphasized her femininity,' she would say in the late 1940s.

'The most difficult aspect of my work is to allow women to move with ease, so they do not have to feel that they are enclosed in a costume. Not having to change their attitude or way of being because of their outfit...And the human body is always in movement.' Gabrielle Chanel

A TIMELESS PIECE

The Chanel suit combined the masculine and feminine and was a perfect reflection of the game the designer had been playing since the early days of her career: the appropriation of the male wardrobe. Karl Lagerfeld would later say, 'The Chanel jacket is actually inspired by an Austrian men's jacket. Coco Chanel invented a type of clothing that did not yet exist in that exact form...it's one of the symbols that defines the Chanel style.' This duality allowed the creation of a timeless piece embodying freedom and elegance. With Chanel, the message is clear: get rid of the superfluous and make clothes flow with a woman's movements so that they do not hinder her in any way.

This revolution may seem insignificant today, but it allowed women in the 1950s to continue their journey of emancipation, including in terms of how they looked. The jacket can be seen as one of the early symbols of the feminist movement, which the couturière was championing without knowing it. Jackie Kennedy, Jane Birkin, Grace Kelly, Romy

The jacket has no darts.

Straight sleeve slightly angled at the elbow, allowing ease of movement.

Trim in frayed tweed.

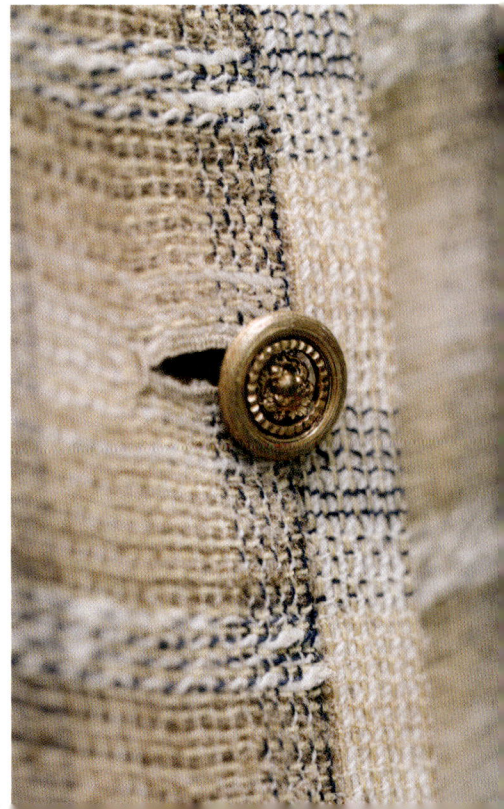

Schneider and many others would all be ambassadors of this iconic garment, which is now also worn by such men as Pharrell Williams.

REINVENTING THE CHANEL JACKET

After Mademoiselle's death in 1971, each year the teams of the fashion house took turns to offer reinterpretations of the iconic jacket, but it was not until the arrival of Karl Lagerfeld in 1983 that it was given a radical new twist. He would continue to reinvent it for almost forty years: whether in short, oversized or sequined versions, the Chanel jacket became a timeless garment produced in never-ending variations.

A SPECIAL STRUCTURE

The jacket has a straight cut and closes edge to edge with buttons usually decorated with the fashion house logo or a lion's head; the bottom of the jacket is weighted with a chain to create a flawless drape. It has no darts at the bust or back; the sleeves are slightly angled, allowing maximum movement of the arm, and are set high on the shoulder. The lining is made from silk.

Another important detail is the trim around the edges, the pocket openings and the ends of the sleeves. The trim can be braided, in grosgrain, frayed tweed or with a feature chain and is one of the most essential elements of Chanel jackets.

MADE TO MEASURE

Chanel did not make sketches for her collections, saying that she was a seamstress and that it was therefore her job to sew. With her models and clients, she would often remove and reset the sleeves on jackets multiple times until she was satisfied that they did sufficient justice to the women wearing them.

Pocket flap with trim.

An important House of Chanel symbol, a lion's head decorates each of the buttons.

Edge-to-edge closure.

Four patch pockets

Laced deep-cut
V-shaped neckline

Belt made
of rings with
a gunmetal
patina

A GARMENT WITH CONNOTATIONS

The roots of the safari jacket date back to the beginning
of the 20th century, when European colonizers in Africa
dressed in a functional way to protect themselves from the
sand, sun and soaring temperatures. A comfortable garment,
it is also reminiscent of the uniforms worn by the British Army
in India. For some, it represents the concept of explorers
conquering new lands while for others it has connotations
of exploitation and oppression.

THE SAFARI JACKET

BY YVES ST LAURENT

Yves Saint Laurent first introduced the saharienne, *or safari jacket, in his 1967 runway shows. However, it was an 'off-collection' design created for a photo shoot in* Vogue *magazine the following year that made the garment famous and quickly turned it into a classic. With the safari jacket, Yves Saint Laurent continued to define his style, which borrowed from male and military codes of dress to revolutionize women's fashion.*

MASCULINE INSPIRATION

The first hints of a safari jacket appeared at Yves Saint Laurent in the Summer 1966 collection, although in a different form from the designer's definitive version, consisting of an ocelot jacket, shirt and cotton leggings. In the summer of 1967, the 'Bambara' collection was themed around Africa and featured 'model 42', more explicitly described as a 'beige canvas safari jacket'. The civil unrest of May 1968 in France redefined the rules around seduction and resulted in a radical overhaul of women's fashion, creating fertile ground for the design of the safari tunic as it was released that year: a short garment in linen or cotton with an endless plunging laced neckline and four patch pockets, worn with a ringed metal belt in a gunmetal patina.

AN ICONIC PIECE

Despite the departure of Yves Saint Laurent in 2002, the creative directors of the fashion house have been happily reinterpreting this timeless piece for over fifty years. Tom Ford, Hedi Slimane and Anthony Vaccarello have all regularly included the iconic garment in their runway shows.

The idea of creating Mademoiselle Joséphine was born from my passion for vintage fashion and my desire to offer an experience based on the authenticity and history of each piece. My father was an expert in decorative art and Art Nouveau and owned a gallery on rue Bonaparte in the 6th arrondissement, and my mother was head of public relations at the Drouot auction house in Paris. Both of them supported me to develop this passion for unique pieces and treasures from the past. Always fascinated by fashion and runway shows as a child, I wanted to create a space where connoisseurs could come and discover treasures: a sanctuary for lovers of vintage. The atmosphere of my boutique located in St-Germain-des-Prés exudes the charm and authenticity of Paris in the 1930s. I carefully curate the items and enjoy promoting more sustainable and eco-friendly fashion. The idea was to capture the essence of the past while also offering a modern vision of fashion.

What is your favourite piece?

A Chanel coat from the Autumn/Winter 1996 collection. This amazing piece is particularly difficult to find, especially in this incredible fuchsia colour. The magnificent buttons on the coat were made by Maison Gripoix and are iconic. The colour adds a vibrant and bold feel, which I absolutely love. And the timeless cut and quality of execution make it a real treasure for lovers of Chanel and vintage fashion. I accessorize this coat with another piece that, although more classic in style, is also iconic: the Kelly Sellier bag in Rouge H box calf leather from the 1960s. For me, this bag is the perfect embodiment of an era rich in superb craftsmanship and timeless legendary pieces.

What is the rarest piece you have sold?

There's no doubt about that one: a reissue of the famous Mondrian dress made by Yves Saint Laurent in 1965. Mine was from the Rive Gauche Spring/Summer 1997 collection. This legendary piece perfectly reflects the fusion between a love of fashion and a love of art, two passions that are very dear to me. The Mondrian dress is a true work of art, inspired by the celebrated paintings of Piet Mondrian. Its bold, striking design featuring blocks of primary colour has made it a fashion icon, symbolizing the inventiveness and innovation of Yves Saint Laurent. I'm really proud to have had the opportunity to offer my clients this rare and prestigious piece, which demonstrates the heritage and cultural importance of fashion in the world of art.

Who are your vintage icons?

Thierry Mugler and Yves Saint Laurent, no question. Their designs have impacted the history of fashion thanks to their bold vision and ability to push the boundaries of aesthetics. Thierry Mugler is famous for his futuristic silhouettes and avant-garde designs that revolutionized the fashion industry in the 1980s and 1990s. His sculptural pieces, oversized shoulders and innovative details captured the imagination of the entire world. On a more personal note, I was brought up with them via his runway shows and my mother's wardrobe.

And Yves Saint Laurent represents timeless elegance and Parisian style. His designs redefined the standards of women's fashion, introducing androgynous silhouettes, tuxedos for women and the fashion codes of men's clothing. His revolutionary style defied convention and ushered in a new era of sophistication and freedom in fashion. As vintage icons, Thierry Mugler and Yves Saint Laurent represent a bygone era of glamour and timeless elegance. Their legacy continues to inspire today's designers, making them essential references for anyone looking for collectible pieces.

What makes your shop special?

I would say my unique approach to vintage and luxury fashion: I only present pieces that I resonate with. I focus on what makes them special, their history and their authenticity. My personal experience in the world of art and auctions allows me to curate rare and unique pieces that are often full of history and emotion. My commitment to more sustainable and eco-friendly fashion, by giving a second life to pre-loved items, adds an ethical dimension to my business.

Who are your customers?

My clientele is diverse and reflects the universal appeal of luxury vintage fashion. My customers include fashion enthusiasts, connoisseurs, collectors and tourists from all over the world...and sometimes simply my neighbours. Famous models and actors looking for unique pieces for their public appearances are also important clients. I'm lucky to have a loyal clientele who resonate with my outlook and taste, allowing us to enjoy a shared passion.

MADEMOISELLE JOSÉPHINE
16 rue des Saints-Pères
75007 Paris
www.mllejosephine.com

LE SMOKING TUXEDO

BY YVES SAINT LAURENT

'Le Smoking was an opportunity for me to give women power by offering them this highly symbolic men's suit.' Yves Saint Laurent's most iconic and timeless garment is undoubtedly the tuxedo.

A SUBVERSIVE PIECE

Eminently subversive, the designer was not the first person to transfer the tuxedo to the female wardrobe. In the 1920s, 'flappers' adopted it as a must-have item, and Elsa Schiaparelli was the first couturière to design a tuxedo jacket for women.

At that time, a French law from 1800 prohibiting women from cross-dressing was still deeply embedded in the French psyche (it was abolished only in 2013). A woman wearing a tuxedo was therefore seen as an affront to morality. In 1930, Marlene Dietrich caused uproar in cinemas when she appeared wearing a tailcoat and top hat in a scene from Josef von Sternberg's film *Morocco*.

THE MUST-HAVE PIECE BY YVES SAINT LAURENT

In his Autumn/Winter 1966 collection, Yves Saint Laurent introduced his most iconic piece: Le Smoking or tuxedo suit. Its name comes from the smoking jacket worn by men in all-male smoking rooms to protect the rest of their clothing from the smell of cigars. Given the purpose of the garment, it was only ever used by men. The Saint Laurent tuxedo is not, however, a copy of a man's piece of clothing: it uses the fashion codes associated with it while adapting them to the female form.

TUXEDO DESIGN CODES

Complemented with a white organza ruffled shirt, bow tie, straight-cut trousers and a satin cummerbund belt, the tuxedo once again threatened to cause uproar, although the craze for the piece was as strong as the shockwaves it sent through the socialite parties where a guest dared to wear it.

A POPULAR SUCCESS?

'The street runs faster than the shows. I noticed this five years ago when I made my first tuxedo. In couture: no success. In ready-to-wear: huge.' It was Yves Saint Laurent's ready-to-wear line Rive Gauche, sold at the rue de Tournon shop in Paris, that generated enthusiasm for the tuxedo. Le Smoking was favoured by celebrities, worn by Françoise Hardy when she visited the United States in 1968, and by Catherine Deneuve at her Parisian parties. The buzz was out, and it soon became impossible to buy a Saint Laurent tuxedo as stores ran out of stock.

We might say that the tuxedo is the feminist counterpart of the little black dress.

A PIECE THAT GAINED LEGENDARY STATUS

In 1975, Helmut Newton reinforced the myth surrounding the piece, when Le Smoking featured in one of the most reproduced photographs in the world. A narrow street at night and a lone woman, Vibeke Knudsen, poses alone, dressed like a dandy, cigarette in hand – a beautiful androgynous creature who seems to come from another era.

Since then, designers around the world have continued to reinterpret the tuxedo, while remaining faithful to the timeless image created by Yves Saint Laurent, sometimes merely hinting at it with just a satin stripe or lapel.

'THE MOMENT WHEN YVES GAVE WOMEN POWER'

This quotation from Pierre Bergé, co-founder of Yves Saint Laurent, explains one of the reasons for the suit's success. The woman of the 1970s is a woman in trousers. Although this transition may seem insignificant, it laid the foundations for the modern, independent businesswoman of the 1980s. We might say that the tuxedo is the feminist counterpart of the little black dress. Extreme in its expression of sensuality, and often seen nowadays worn next to the skin, the versatility of this masculine/feminine garment makes it a timeless and classic design.

In the Yves Saint Laurent Autumn/Winter 2023 collection, creative director Anthony Vaccarello gave the tuxedo pride of place in his runway show: 60 years after its release, fashion cannot do without Le Smoking, and its various iterations live on in wardrobes around the world.

ʃatin lapels

On the original men's smoking jacket, satin lapels allowed ash and embers to easily slide off, protecting the garment from unsightly burn marks. There are two types of tuxedo jacket: the first, known as the Deauville, is single-breasted with one button. The Capri is double-breasted and has two or three pairs of buttons. In both cases, they can have either a shawl collar or a notched collar.

STRIPE

The lower half of the tuxedo usually features a satin stripe that echoes the lapels and is positioned on the sides of trousers and skirts.

Infinite iterations

The tuxedo jacket was originally worn with trousers. It was so successful that Saint Laurent continued to make infinite variations for each season's fashion show, including skirts, dresses, jumpsuits and tuxedo shorts.

THE BAR JACKET

In 1947, Carmel Snow, editor-in-chief of Harper's Bazaar *famously labelled Christian Dior's first couture collection the 'New Look'. The term was subsequently more widely used to define the designs of the House of Dior in the post-war period. After years of austerity, Christian Dior designed clothing that initially caused uproar: he rejected the codes of post-war fashion by offering women a highly structured suit jacket that would allow them to regain control of their silhouette.*

A WHIFF OF SCANDAL

The understated, simple cuts and colours and limited quantities of material used at that time were suddenly replaced by a more sumptuous form of fashion that championed premium materials, modern cuts and endless rolls of fabric. It is easy to understand the shock that this vastly different collection must have created: the change in volumes, the extreme elegance of the outfits combined with the technicality required to make them, and the unseemly amount of fabric used.

'SLIM DOWN THE BODY WITHOUT LOSING THE WAIST'

The first Dior collection was known as 'Corolle' and was shown at 30 avenue Montaigne in Paris. One model clearly stood out from the rest, the Bar suit: a peplum jacket in natural shantung paired with a pleated skirt. The technicality of this piece of afternoon wear was worthy of an architectural design.

   The young Pierre Cardin, head of the atelier in the new fashion house, was responsible for the proportions of the garment, which took its name from the bar of the Plaza Athénée Hotel where Christian Dior liked to have a drink at the end of a working day. He bought sheets of surgical cotton and folded them accordion-style to add volume to the skirt, as he found that the peplums would collapse without it. Legend has it that Christian Dior himself took a hammer to his cardboard mannequins to create the shapes he wanted. The jacket was the star outfit of the runway show, and an icon was born.

'The lines of this
first Spring collection
are typically feminine
and made to enhance
the beauty of the women
who wear them.'
Christian Dior, designer notes for his first
runway show, February 1947.

GIVING WOMEN BACK THEIR BODIES

The Bar jacket would be immortalized in a photograph taken on the banks of the Seine, when model Renée Breton improvised a beautifully theatrical pose. Full of self-confidence, she seems to hold the world in the palm of her hand.

And this was very much the idea of the designer: to create outfits that allowed women to reclaim the femininity of their silhouettes. The jacket allowed Dior's upmarket customers, and the many women who went in search of a 'Dior-style jacket', to reappropriate both their bodies and the image of themselves that had been created by the Second World War. Each collection was intended to result in a categorical change of silhouette.

Unfortunately, the designer remained at the head of his fashion house for only ten years. Nonetheless, his jacket has continued to be reinterpreted by its successive creative directors. The Bar jacket has become an iconic model of the House of Dior and doubtless still has many wonderful years ahead of it.

THE WORK OF AN ARCHITECT

It took around 500 hours of work to complete the jacket, which seemed to have been moulded directly on to the bodies of the women who wore it. The skirt alone required 14m of fabric.

'Dior thought he was presenting a cautious collection, but the reclaimed voluptuousness of the shapes, the generous volumes of the fabrics, the extended lengths of the skirts and dresses, after all those years of deprivation, were quite literally shocking.'
Olivier Saillard

HERMÈS PARIS

THE SILK SCARF

BY HERMÈS

Known as a carré (the French for square), the Hermès scarf can be traced back to the neckerchiefs worn by men in the 19th century, including soldiers who donned them as military badges. In 1937, on the advice of fashion designer Lola Prusac, Robert Dumas created the first Hermès scarf to mark the centenary of the fashion house. The design was known as 'Jeu des Omnibus et Dames Blanches', inspired by a popular French board game of the late 1820s. It also celebrated the inauguration of the first bus line in Paris, connecting la Madeleine to la Bastille.

THE ORIGIN OF THE 'PAPILLON'

The scarf had clearly defined specifications: 90 × 90cm in silk twill (nearly 500km of thread were required to make it), with rolled edges for an absolutely perfect finish. Robert Dumas was also fascinated by innovative textile-printing techniques. He started out by designing military, equestrian and sea-related themes.

Today, silk from Brazil is woven at Perrin & Fils using a special technique that allows it to be printed on. A very particular type of silk is used, made from the eggs of *Bombyx mori*, a moth originally native to Asia. Silkworms from the moth lay 300 eggs over their lifetime, and this is the number required to make one scarf. Hermès therefore refers to its square scarves as 'papillons' (*papillon de nuit* is the French for moth).

A TIMELESS CLASSIC

Over more than 80 years, 1,500 designs of the square scarf have been created by artists such as Cassandre, Xavier de Poret and Robert Dallet. During the printing process, between 400 and 600 hours of work are required for the engravers to complete a project. The fashion house is able to draw on 75,000 different colours.

Worn by Grace Kelly as a sling to support her injured arm, by Brigitte Bardot as a headdress, and with oversized sunglasses by Jackie Kennedy, the scarf benefited from continuous publicity in the 1950s and 1960s. It was so popular that it became the classic gift to give a French girl.

Scarf in printed silk brocade with 'Feux d'artifices' (Fireworks) design. Created by Michel Duchêne in 1987 to celebrate the 150th anniversary of Hermès. The scarf was reissued in 1993.

Printed silk scarf with green and red borders: 'À la Gloire de la Légion Etrangère' (To the Glory of the Foreign Legion) by Hugo Grygkar. Design from 1959.

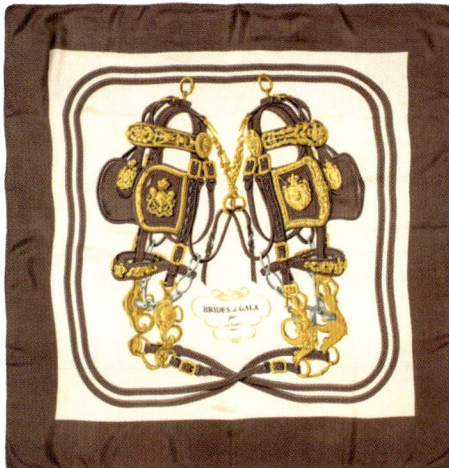

Printed silk scarf with brown border: 'Brides de Gala' (Gala Bridles) by Hugo Grygkar. Design from 1959.

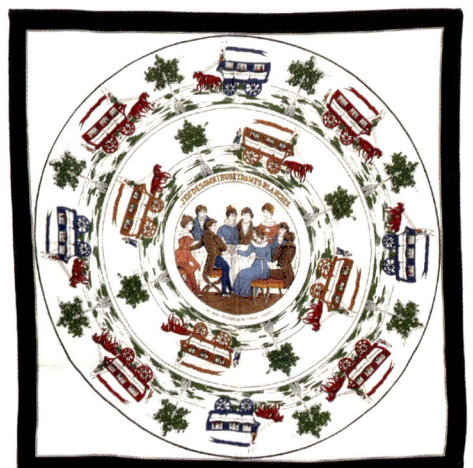

The first Hermès scarf, 'Jeu des Omnibus et Dames Blanches', by Robert Dumas. Design from 1937.

DIFFERENT WAYS OF WEARING A *CARRÉ*

Shunned for many years because it was seen as old-fashioned, the Hermès scarf has made a strong comeback and is now worn as a belt, top and skirt, or tied in the hair. Expanding scarf designs beyond strictly equestrian themes has meant that the scarf appeals to a vast range of customers, making it one of the most important products in the Hermès catalogue. The fashion house has also developed 70 × 70cm and 140 × 140cm versions to meet every kind of need.

Its most recent success is the Twilly, a narrow silk scarf that customers primarily use to tie around the handles of their handbags for a customized look.

Carré worn as a belt.

Carré worn as a headscarf.

THE TRENCH COAT

BY BURBERRY

A global fashion icon famous for its tartan motif, the trench coat can be traced back to 1856, when Thomas Burberry, a young gentleman's outfitter, started to create rainproof clothing that also wicked away perspiration. He stood out from his competitors with an innovative technology that involved waterproofing each cotton and wool fibre before making an item, rather than treating the finished garment.

A NEW NECESSARY AND USEFUL COAT

Proving enormously popular with anyone working in jobs exposed to the elements, the modest Burberrys retail outlet became a department store in 1870, specializing in warm, waterproof and comfortable clothing. Burberrys then revolutionized the world of coats with the invention of gabardine, the most breathable fabric at the time.

MILITARY ROOTS

The trench coat was an expensive product, and the soldiers who wore it in the trenches of the First World War were mainly wealthy officers. It therefore became an identifier of social class. The double-breasted coat, fitted at the waist and falling below the knee in a flared cut, was eminently utilitarian, featuring deep pockets, sleeves with tightening tabs at the wrists, and a belt fitted with D-rings for attaching accessories. It would gradually shed its military image and appeal to all sections of society.

THE EMBODIMENT OF STYLE

Hollywood greatly facilitated the transition of the trench coat to a timeless classic: in 1942, Humphrey Bogart wore it as an intrepid gentleman in the film *Casablanca*; Marlene Dietrich sported the coat as a sublime femme fatale in *A Foreign Affair* in 1948, and Audrey Hepburn wore it as the elegant seductress in *Breakfast at Tiffany's* in 1961. The trench coat immediately became a classic in the British male wardrobe: the best ally of gentlemen everywhere, it was the perfect embodiment of British style.

Haymarket check tartan
by Burberry.

INVENTION OF A PATTERN

The Haymarket check, Burberry's signature print, was first used in the 1920s on the inside of raincoats such as the trench coat, but it was only in 1960 that it became an iconic must-have when thousands of customers began asking for 'Burberry checks'.

DIVERSIFICATION OF SHAPES AND PATTERNS

In 1967, an inspired buyer used her coat lining to wrap and protect a piece of luggage during the presentation of a collection: this marked the start of the check pattern appearing on accessories, suitcases, umbrellas and scarves and, later, ready-to-wear lines.

Such global fame and popular recognition has inspired designers from around the world: Martin Margiela, Rei Kawakubo and Jean Paul Gaultier have all reinterpreted the trench coat in their own way.

The House of Burberry has continued to evolve and pursue the tradition of innovation championed by the brand's founder, who died in 1926. The Rainbow check pattern released in 2018 celebrated LGBTQIA+ diversity, with a nod to the rainbow integrated into the legendary tartan motif.

Cap with Rainbow check pattern.

In 1999, the fashion house modified its name, with the final 's' disappearing under the pencil stroke of art director Fabien Baron.

Men's raincoat with transparent effect and visible lining, created by Riccardo Tisci, chief creative officer at Burberry from 2018.

THE RED DRESS

Red is to Valentino what black is to Chanel. Valentino Garavani constantly reinterpreted his iconic designs but always in the same shade of his instantly recognizable red, a colour as visually powerful as a logo.

THE COLOUR OF DESIRE

In the West, red is the first colour that humans mastered, both in terms of painting and dyeing. This is probably why it continued to be the quintessential colour for so long, and the richest from a material, social, artistic, dreamworld and symbolic point of view.

Since ancient times, red has also been a more ambivalent symbol of fire, blood, danger and violence. It was also synonymous with passion and sexuality as well as with extreme suffering. The couturier embraced these multiple meanings, combining both glamour and temptation in his sensual designs.

THE CREATION OF A SYMBOL

After stints with Jean Dessès and Guy Laroche, Valentino quickly set up his own fashion house in Rome in 1959. In his very first collection, the Fiesta dress (the last piece in the show) blended a vibrant red with reflections of the setting sun: Valentino red was born. Celebrities around the world made it one of their favourite colours to walk the red carpet, creating a powerful sense of visual continuity.

Despite the designer's departure in 2009, Maria Grazia Chiuri and Pierpaolo Piccioli have continued to make *Rosso Valentino* – Valentino Red – a symbol of the fashion house.

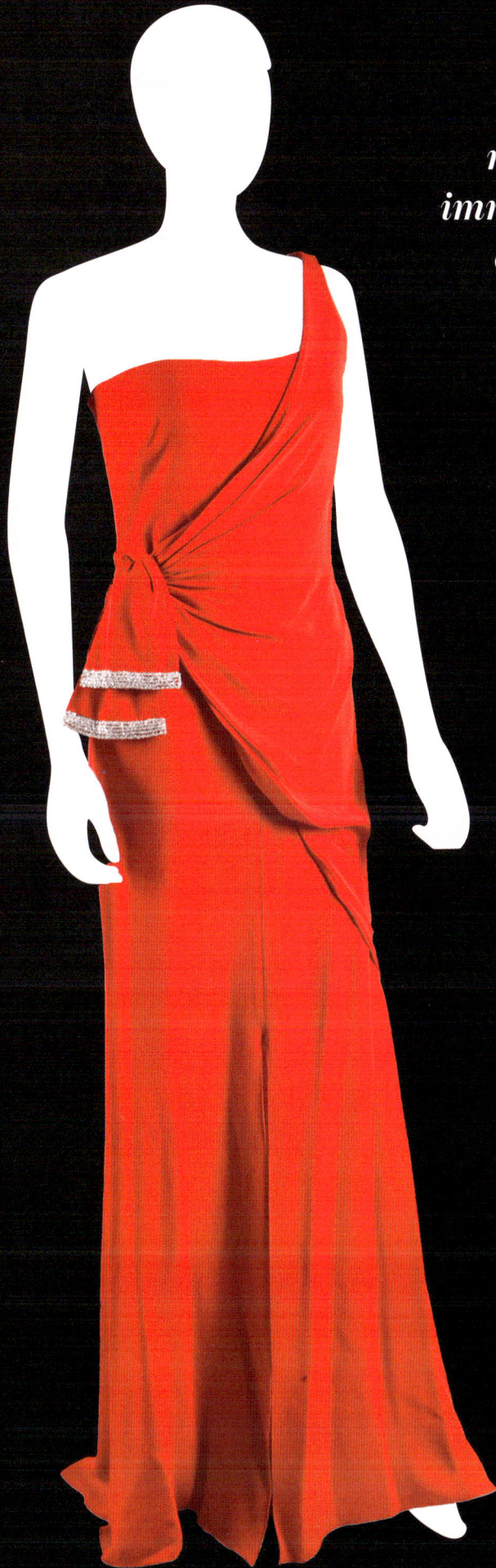

'*For the House of Valentino, red is not just a colour. It is an immutable sign, a logo, an iconic element of the brand, a value.*'
Valentino Garavani

'Sailor jerseys go with everything. They never go out of style and probably never will.'

Jean Paul Gaultier

THE MARINIÈRE

BY JEAN PAUL GAULTIER

Originally, a marinière referred to a plain white shirt with a wide boat neck. Made of jersey, it was worn by French sailors (marins) at the beginning of the 19th century. In 1858, a white jersey with blue stripes became the official uniform of the French Navy.

THE ORIGINS OF AN ICONIC PIECE

In 1916, Gabrielle Chanel took this masculine garment and incorporated it into her own outfits, although, ironically, she never transposed it into her collections. In 1962, Yves Saint Laurent included it in his 'Matelot' (sailor) collection.

BY JEAN PAUL GAULTIER

Jean Paul Gaultier presented the *marinière* for the first time in his 1976 runway show, but it was not until 1983 that it became a recurring theme with his first men's ready-to-wear collection 'Boy Toy'. His passion for the garment was such that he designed it for both women and men, and even went so far as to decorate the bottle of his Le Male fragrance with it. The creation of this masculine ideal turned the *marinière* into a sensual symbol, both manly and sensitive at the same time.

The timeless *marinière* is reinterpreted each year by many different designers but has never reflected the essence of a fashion house in quite the way it does at Jean Paul Gaultier.

PRECISE SPECIFICATIONS

On 27 March 1858, a French decree was drawn up stating that the *marinière* was now the official uniform of sailors. It stipulated that the top should have precisely 21 white and 20 indigo stripes.

A *marinière* in mesh, a material championed by the designer. A hanging loop (detail, right), typical of Gaultier, is attached to the back of the garment.

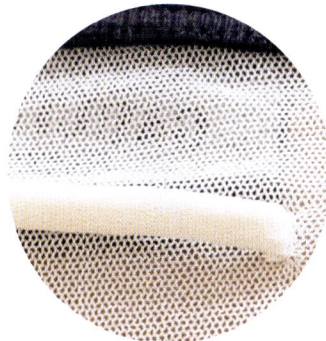

THE VERSEAU LINE

BY AZZARO

The Verseau line is particularly representative of the work of Italian designer Loris Azzaro. His Lurex and chain tops were created in the 1960s in a multitude of colours. Verseau is the French for the star sign Aquarius.

A JEWELLERY DESIGNER

Loris Azzaro made his debut in 1965, although not in fashion design but costume jewellery, which he first made for his wife as a substitute for the jewels she coveted in shop windows. These early designs laid the foundations for the Verseau line. Azzaro started to get orders for other pieces of jewellery, too. At the same time, he began designing beaded bags and dazzling Lurex mini-tops. He founded his fashion house in 1967 and quickly became successful, with big names such as Tina Turner, Liza Minnelli and Jane Birkin buying his sensual and elegant pieces in the 1970s.

A SIMPLE AND ELEGANT TIMELESS CLASSIC

In 2010, Vanessa Paradis became the ambassador for the line. Now considered a timeless piece, this top has become iconic despite its technical simplicity featuring rows of varnished chains mounted on a Lurex mesh.

Round sleeves

Colour-coordinated varnished chains

Lurex mesh

THE *SKATER DRESS*

BY AZZEDINE ALAÏA

Azzedine Alaïa is known as the 'surgeon' of couture as his outfits mould perfectly to the body like a second skin. It is difficult to choose just one iconic piece by the couturier, given the wide diversity of the brand's DNA.

THE ICONIC SKATER DRESS

The skater dress could be considered *the* signature model of the fashion house because of the media exposure it received from the 1980s to the present: it has been worn by women as famous as Michelle Obama, Khloé Kardashian, Oprah Winfrey and many others. More than just a dress, it embodies the style the designer made timeless.

SELECT COLLECTIONS

After brief stints at Christian Dior and Guy Laroche, and with the help of Thierry Mugler, Azzedine Alaïa founded his fashion house in 1964 on rue de Bellechasse in Paris. He would stay there until 1984. As a genuine 'incubator' of trends, he launched his first collections by showing them at his home and selling pieces by word of mouth only. Top models from around the world – Linda Evangelista, Christy Turlington and Naomi Campbell – all rushed to walk the 'runway' in his apartment, wanting no payment from the designer but hoping that he would gift them the pieces they had worn (which left the world's press speechless).

'I make clothes, women make fashion.'
Azzedine Alaïa

A SIGNATURE

From the designer's very beginnings, one fabric stands out as the signature of the fashion house: stretch knit, or more precisely the 'bandage knit', which, although it was used from 1983, first became a big hit in the Spring/Summer 1990 collection. The 1980s marked a turning point: celebrities from all over the world such as Grace Jones and Tina Turner wore designs that became legendary symbols of the fashion house thanks to their visual power. How could anyone forget the dress made from the French flag draped around opera singer Jessye Norman for the 200th anniversary of the French Revolution in 1989? Or the collection that made headlines in 1991 with its 'TATI' prints, reflecting the designer's wish to combine a couture fashion house with the least expensive French brand of the time?

Although the label always sought to stay under the radar, iconic elements such as eyelets, mesh, lacing and ideas inspired by corsetry are immediately recognizable and identifiable as belonging to the world of Azzedine Alaïa.

The skater dress was created in the 1980s. Worn high on the waist, the skirt flares to mid-thigh level, making it suitable for all body shapes. It is now an iconic piece from the fashion house. ▶

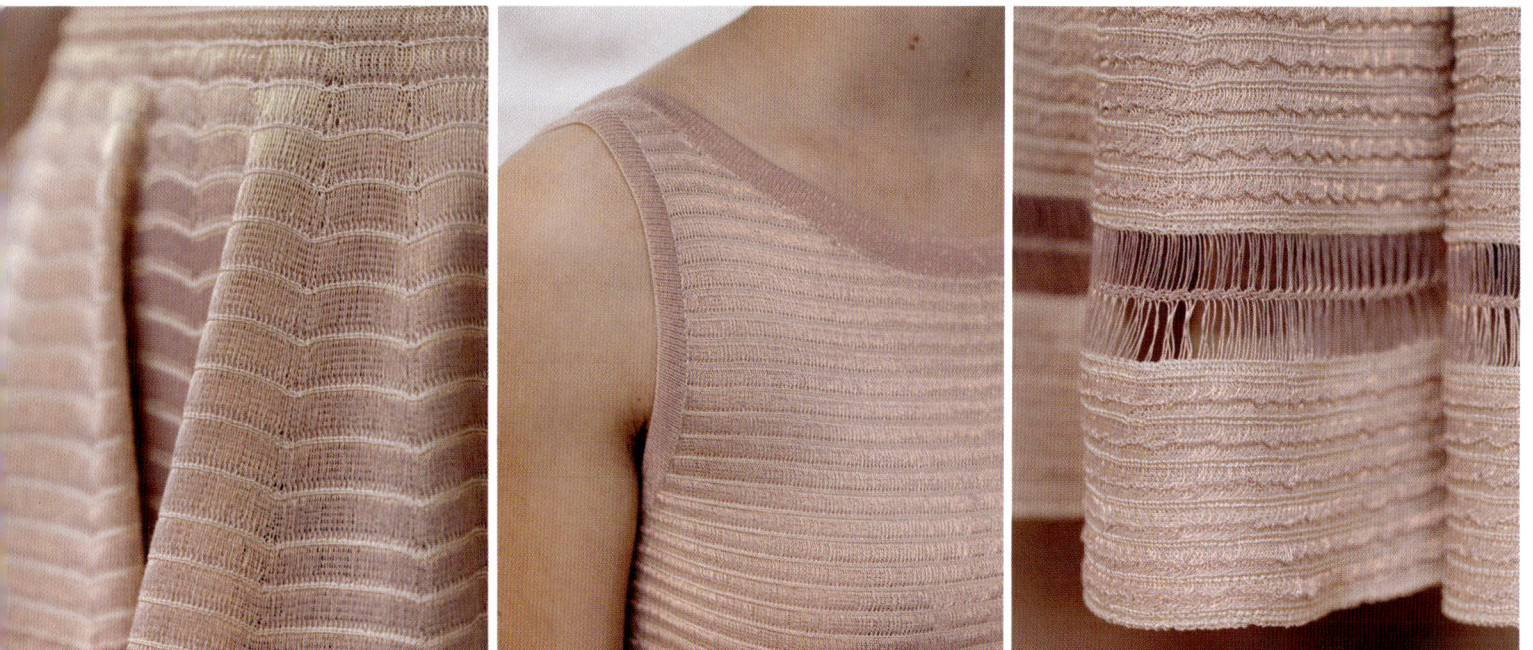

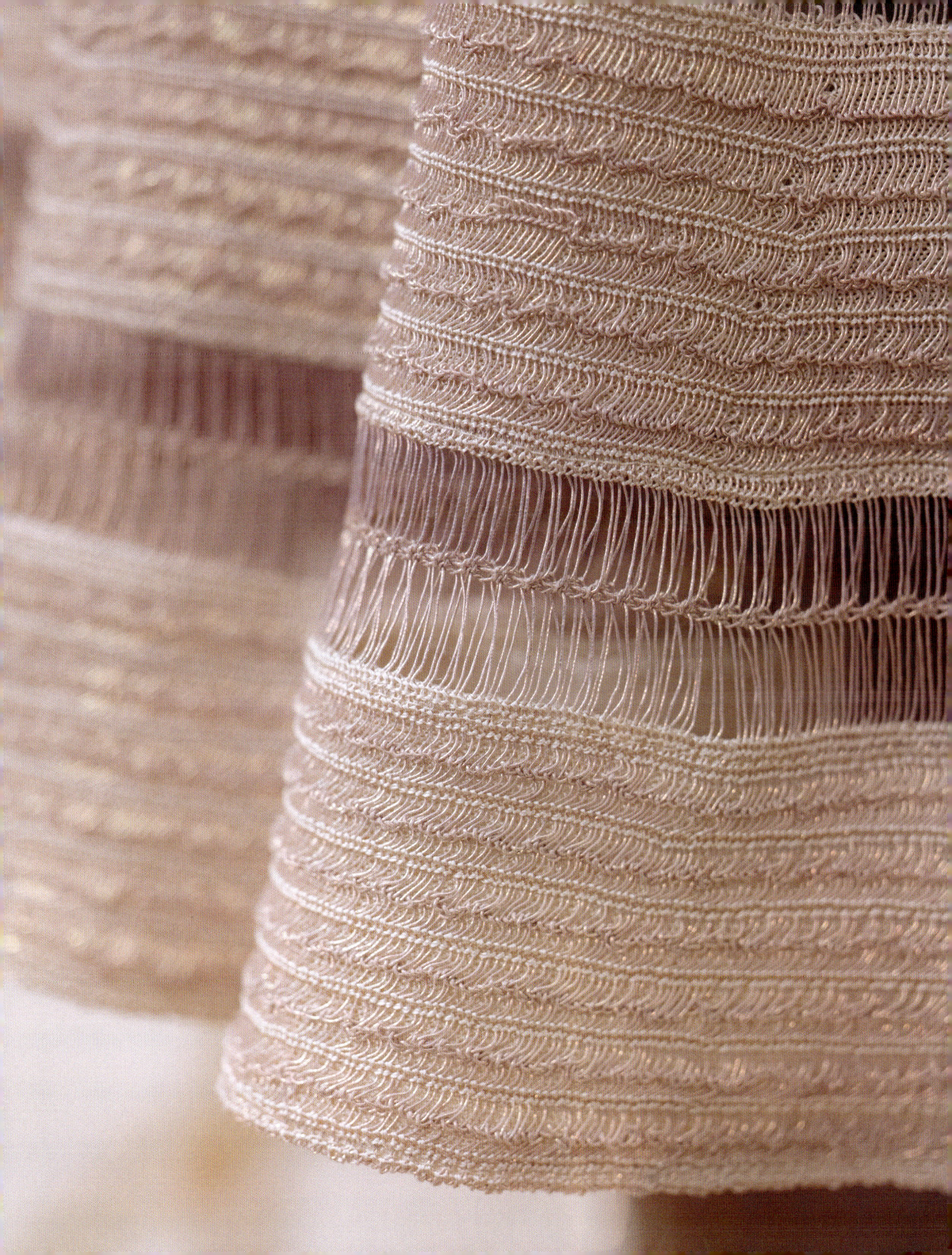

For his Spring/Summer 1991 collection, Azzedine Alaïa wanted to use the famous pink-and-white houndstooth print of budget brand Tati. In exchange for this agreement, Tati asked the couturier to design some exclusive pieces for the brand. He created a pair of sneakers, a dress, a bag and a T-shirt, and in return gave himself the freedom of using the pattern on numerous pieces in his runway show. All the top models of the time sported this look on the runway.

RE/EE

ReSee is an online platform selling exclusive and authentic pre-loved fashion and luxury handbags. It was founded in 2013 by two fashion veterans, Sofia Bernardin and Sabrina Marshall, from *Vogue* and *Self Service Magazine*, respectively. Their vision is to include luxury fashion in the circular economy. Each ReSee piece is curated by professionals, authenticated by experts, and restored by artisans where necessary. And their mission – to find special pieces with a unique story that will make each customer feel wonderful about themselves.

What is your favourite piece?

We're absolutely fascinated by Nicolas Ghesquière. We were lucky enough to have one of his incredible corset dresses from the iconic Spring/Summer 2008 collection. This piece was the second look of the show. It was made of Neoprene with a floral print. It was worn by Jennifer Connelly, one of Ghesquière's muses, at a premiere in 2007, and featured in the February 2008 'Spring Forward' issue of British *Vogue*, photographed by Patrick Demarchelier.

'We want to include luxury fashion in the circular economy.'

What is the rarest piece you have sold?

There really isn't a rare piece that we haven't sold. Major collectors are particularly interested in these. It's harder to source them than to sell them.

Who are your vintage icons?

The most iconic brand for us is undoubtedly Yves Saint Laurent. We started ReSee with a collection of over 200 Saint Laurent vintage pieces, mostly from the 1970s. Yves Saint Laurent was the first couturier to introduce ready-to-wear into the luxury sector and his designs liberated women of the time. His genius made him future-proof and his vintage pieces are just as modern and stylish now as they were back then.

How is your business different from others? What's special about it?

We take immense pride in our curation, knowledge and expertise. ReSee is a group of people who are passionate about fashion and its history. Sofia and I are always keen to highlight historic moments in fashion and celebrate great achievements like Prada's 'Fairies' collection or Phoebe Philo's tenure at Celine.

Who are your typical customers?

ReSee customers are women who don't want just anything in their wardrobe. They want pieces that will last and give them a sense of independence throughout their lives.

What is your favourite vintage piece?

Our first purchase at ReSee was a 1988 Alaïa fringed jacket. We'll never get rid of it!

RESEE
48bis avenue Kléber
75116 Paris
www.resee.com

THE DISC DRESS

BY PACO RABANNE

Salvador Dalí famously said, 'There are only two geniuses in Spain: me and Paco Rabanne.' His words are an accurate reflection of both men — daring, flamboyant and nonconformist. Rabanne, who was raised in France and trained as an architect, did not think of himself as a clothes designer. This is no doubt why Gabrielle Chanel dubbed this inimitable inventor 'the metallurgist'. The irreverent Rabanne replaced the usual threads and needles of fashion with pliers, rivets and blowtorches from the very beginning of his career. He conceptualized his garments in the same way that he made architectural drawings, and then welded and assembled in the style of a construction worker.

'UNWEARABLE DRESSES'

From 1965, Paco Rabanne collaborated on the creation of accessories made from Rhodoid (a type of plastic) for a collection known as 'Pacotilles', which included earrings and sunglasses. He transposed this material on to the designs of his first collection, 'Manifesto', on 1 February 1966. Here he presented 'Twelve Unwearable Dresses in Contemporary Materials', the ultimate example of what was then known as futuristic fashion. His now-famous disc dress was also shown in this collection for the first time.

'A naked woman under a metal garment is both available and inaccessible, and that is the essence of eroticism.'

Paco Rabanne

'Fashion is freedom...Why not leather, Rhodoid, paper or another material in the future? I think it's absolutely ridiculous to continue dressing women in fabric as we did in the 19th century.' Paco Rabanne

Rhodoid dress
Rhodoid was invented in 1917 and is the brand name of a transparent, non-combustible cellulose-acetate material.

Metal dress
Dress with rivets and rings.

Heart-shaped disc dress
A dress made of white heart-shaped discs, linked together by silver-tone metal chains, created in the 1970s. The signature of the fashion house is displayed on a metal plate at the top of the back.

THE REVOLUTION OF 1966

The disc dress revealed all of the body; there was no longer any possibility of concealment or secrets. The metal dresses were assembled using rivets and rings. The innovative designer also presented them against a soundtrack, creating the first ever runway show with music. The first metal dress was issued in 1966: a mini dress made of aluminium plates connected with rings. It symbolized a meeting between the past and future where established fashion codes were turned upside down.

ARMOUR FOR WOMEN'S BODIES

When asked about his dresses in 1976, Rabanne assured the interviewer that metal was the ultimate symbol of femininity. 'It's a silvery, lunar piece of clothing. A naked woman under a metal garment is both available and inaccessible, and that is the essence of eroticism,' he said. He likened his metal clothing to 'armour' and said he wanted to 'make women warriors' by dressing them in it. 'With this armour, they're attempting to win their independence from men. It's highly symbolic and in perfect harmony with the times,' he explained.

Stars from all over the world rushed to get their hands on the latest Paco Rabanne pieces. Françoise Hardy was the standard-bearer for the brand, wearing the 'most expensive dress in the world' in 1968. Made of solid gold and set with diamonds, it weighed an astonishing 38kg.

The architect-couturier of excess cannot be fitted into any box and was a completely new influence on fashion. He even went as far as selling DIY dress kits delivered in small suitcases that customers assembled themselves. His iconic disc dresses in aluminium and Rhodoid are still as fresh as ever and particularly sought after.

OPULENCE LUXURY & VINTAGE

Interview with Raúl Barràgan Sanz

How did you come up with the idea of creating Opulence Luxury & Vintage?

It's been almost ten years since Opulence Luxury & Vintage was founded and...what an adventure!

Opulence Luxury & Vintage now has three separate stores and a showroom. It all started with a personal desire. I wanted to track down rare vintage fashion and decorative pieces, at first only for myself, and then for friends.

Things grew little by little, with people starting to make specific requests. I eventually decided to leave my job and opened a store offering a unique vintage selection of high-end Louis Vuitton, Chanel and Hermès pieces. I opened my second boutique a few years later.

At first, I only wanted to focus on accessories (bags, jewellery and so on) but I gradually developed an interest in clothing (there are so many pretty pieces to offer customers in the world of fashion!), which made me decide to open a third boutique near place Vendôme [a fourth shop has followed]. Here, we offer a wide selection of ready-to-wear attire. This development has allowed us to considerably expand our range of designer labels and discover wonderful new things: for example, I love Moschino and its amazingly funny designs.

What is your favourite current piece?

It's hard to choose just one piece, so I'll give you two.

The first would be the Chanel Vanity Bag in denim from the 1996 collection, which is in particularly good condition. I think denim bags are extraordinarily elegant. They can be equally sublime worn on the arm or placed decoratively on a dressing table or in a walk-in wardrobe.

My second favourite piece would be the Louis Vuitton × Azzedine Alaïa bag, created in 1996 to commemorate the centenary of Monogram canvas. I love animal prints and pieces that reference the animal world in general; this bag is also very difficult to find in the excellent condition of the one we have here.

What is the rarest piece you have sold?

I would say a Louis Vuitton pétanque set in natural leather and in excellent condition, as I've never come across it again. I sometimes find myself imagining my customer playing pétanque in his garden with that set!

Why did you choose to work with vintage pieces?

There's nothing quite like finding a vintage piece in excellent condition, and realizing how it has travelled through the decades to get to us. It's also really interesting to observe the transformation in lifestyles and attitudes through the evolution of clothing, bags and accessories.

What do your stores have that others don't?

I only work with pieces in excellent condition, which are always checked and authenticated. We offer items that are difficult to find elsewhere, and that's why our loyal customers often come back, in search of new and amazing pieces.

Do you have a typical client profile?

Because our boutiques are in the centre of Paris, our clientele tends to be made up of foreign tourists looking for a beautiful vintage piece to take home as an unforgettable souvenir of their trip. Purchases made while on holiday in Paris definitely give them a unique experience because the pieces we offer are very difficult to find in the United States and Asia.

OPULENCE LUXURY & VINTAGE
The four stores are located in Paris in the 2nd, 4th and 11th arrondissements.
• 107 rue Réaumur
• 3 rue Jean du Bellay
• 20 rue Danielle Casanova
• 11 rue Oberkampf
www.opulencevintage.com
Instagram: @opulencevintage

Louis Vuitton pétanque set in natural leather and Monogram canvas.

'I have always been passionate about lines. I redo my drawing 500 times to check the accuracy of the idea and to respect the architecture of the foot.'

Roger Vivier

Low heels

Square metal buckle

THE BELLE VIVIER

BY ROGER VIVIER

Roger Vivier was one of the most gifted shoe designers of the 20th century.
We owe almost all modern forms of the shoe to him.

VIVIER FOR DIOR

Following the success of his first shoe designs, Roger Vivier opened his own store on rue Royale in Paris in 1937. However, it was not until his collaboration with Christian Dior in 1953 that his fame reached dazzling new heights. In that year, the couturier opened a shoe department and hired the shoemaker as a designer. After a number of years dedicated solely to the design of haute couture footwear, Christian Dior was keen to expand into production of ready-to-wear shoes. It was the first and only time that the couturier associated his name with another designer, and the shoes were signed Christian Dior and Roger Vivier on the foothed. This collaboration lasted for ten years, ending in 1963.

THE CRAFTSMAN OF THE FOOT

During this period, Roger Vivier was also busy experimenting with many different types of heel. His famous designs included the Choc heel in 1959, the Comma heel, which became the trademark of his own label from 1963, and the first-ever thigh-length boots.

In 1965, fashion designer Yves Saint Laurent released his new collection entitled 'Mondrian' and asked Roger Vivier to design a striking pump. This was the origin of the black patent-leather shoe with a square silver buckle and low heel. Despite its huge success, it was not until the release of Luis Buñuel's 1967 film *Belle de jour* that the pumps became iconic, when Catherine Deneuve stole the show wearing the famous square-buckle shoes. Today considered the signature model of the brand, the shoes were poetically renamed the Belle Vivier, in homage to the woman who made them famous.

THE STILETTO STAR!

In 1954, Roger Vivier invented the modern stiletto heel, a design that would become hugely popular.

'We leave in the morning with a beige and black pair, we lunch in beige and black, we go to a cocktail party with beige and black. We are dressed from morning to night.'

Gabrielle Chanel

The heel measures 5cm in height: Gabrielle Chanel considered this to be the ideal size, offering both elegance and perfect comfort.

The beige colour lengthens the leg while the black colour shortens the foot and protects the tip of the pump.

THE ſLINGBACK

It was 1937 when Gabrielle Chanel first donned what would become an icon of the fashion house: the two-tone beige shoe with a black toe. Almost 20 years before its official launch, it appeared on the feet of the designer, matching her signature black-and-white outfit as she spent time in the company of Serge Lifar, the star dancer of the Ballets Russes.

MASSARO–CHANEL

In 1957, a few weeks before presenting her new collection, the couturière asked the luxury shoe brand Massaro to make a pair of two-tone slingback pumps. Mademoiselle had a very precise idea of what she wanted. She specified a pair of kidskin pumps that would create an optical illusion: the beige would lengthen the leg while the black tip would make the foot appear smaller. The heel would be 5cm, the perfect height for elegance and comfort, the guiding principles of Chanel.

Raymond Massaro, the grandson of the brand's founder, came up with a model to meet her requirements. It was immediately worn on the feet of some of the most famous women of the time: Catherine Deneuve, Brigitte Bardot and Romy Schneider.

TWO-TONE

Gabrielle Chanel had always loved two-tone colour schemes, often simultaneously wearing one clip-on pearl earring in white and the other one in grey. In the 1950s, convention dictated that shoes should be monochrome and matched to the wearer's suit. A fervent believer in modernity and emancipation, Chanel would apply these concepts to all of her creations.

THE SLINGBACK BY KARL LAGERFELD

As soon as he took over at the helm of Chanel in 1983, Karl Lagerfeld reinterpreted the slingback: he gave it a wider heel and replaced the iconic kidskin with tweed and denim. In 1986, the designer went further and developed the cult two-tone ballet flat, a direct legacy of the slingback.

A SMART SHOE

The strap on the penny loafer contained a notch that allowed Ivy League students to slip a coin inside so that they always had change to call their parents or catch the bus.

The horsebit

The horsebit is omnipresent at Gucci: it can be found on bags, belts and scarves. It is one of the brand's hallmark symbols, playing the same role as the 'H' at Hermès.

The Gucci label

These shoes are the perfect representation of a relaxed, Italian-inspired way of life – the famous *dolce vita* – and also symbolize Florentine style.

THE HORSEBIT LOAFER

BY GUCCI

The 1953 Horsebit loafer was first released...in 1953! The famous leather goods maker and founder of the fashion house, Guccio Gucci, passed away that year. Also in 1953, one of his heirs, Aldo Gucci, decided to launch a shoe line. The Florentine brand had recently entered the American market and, while in the United States, Aldo Gucci noticed the prevalence of loafers. The first model created was a men's loafer topped with a metal horsebit detail.

A VERY SPECIAL TECHNIQUE

The shoe has precise technical specifications: a soft and wonderfully comfortable leather, an upper topped with a metal horsebit design (directly inspired by the equestrian world that Aldo Gucci was so fond of) and 20mm heels. The sole has three nails to prevent wear as it is relatively thin, and a Blake stitch construction. This is a single row of stitching that attaches the upper (top part of the shoe), the insole and the outsole. This process makes the shoe more flexible and also results in lower production costs.

HISTORIC LOAFERS

The 1953 Horsebit loafer was the first item in a man's wardrobe to be identifiable at first glance. From Rome to Hollywood, they were worn for some thirty years by all the stars, from Alain Delon to Dustin Hoffman, as well as Fred Astaire, Clark Gable, Federico Fellini, John F. Kennedy and even Jodie Foster. It was not until 1968 that the fashion house offered its first pair for women. And in 1973, the shoe achieved icon status when the now-famous loafers joined the permanent collections of the Metropolitan Museum of Art in New York and were exhibited there in 1985.

Since 1953, the model has undergone minor modifications, but the basic design remains unchanged. In 2015, Alessandro Michele offered a contemporary version in mule form with the release of the Princetown.

The Chanel signature appears on both the back of the watch and the clasp.

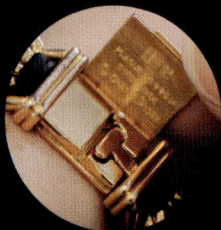

The two-tone finish of the watch is enhanced by a crown set with an onyx cabochon. This two-colour design can also be found on Chanel's Slingback shoes, finished with a black toe.

THE PREMIÈRE

Launched in 1987 under the direction of Jacques Helleu (artistic director of beauty and watch lines at the fashion house until his death in 2007), the elegant and sophisticated Première watch combines the two most iconic Chanel symbols: the intertwined chain of the Classic Flap bag and the stopper of its No. 5 perfume bottle, which replicates the geometry of place Vendôme in Paris.

A WATCH FOR WOMEN

The Première watch was designed to enhance the look of women with a new accessory (even if Gabrielle Chanel never wore a watch herself); it also aimed to propel the brand into the still predominantly masculine world of watchmaking. With a watch designed and created for women instead of a scaled-down version of a men's model, Chanel had made its intentions clear!

INÈS DE LA FRESSANGE AS MUSE

To achieve its objective, the brand opened two new shops for the launch of the Première: in Paris, on the super-chic avenue Montaigne, and in Geneva, Switzerland, the capital of the global watchmaking industry. Inès de La Fressange, the then face of Chanel, was the perfect ambassador of the new watch, for which the fashion house had great ambitions.

GOLD AND BLACK

The timepiece features two colours: gold and black. The gold-plated case houses a black lacquered dial without numerals or indices, around which two gold hands gracefully turn.

THE PREMIÈRE WATCH TODAY

The Première has become the classic Chanel watch, regardless of the variant it comes in. The octagonal case is the only unchanging feature, unlike the bracelet, dial and cabochon, which have been continuously reinterpreted.

Première Originale

In gold-plated steel and yellow gold with an interlaced bracelet, this is faithful to the 1987 model.

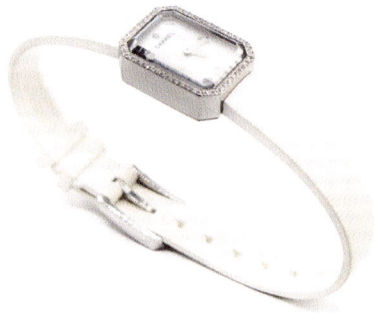

Première Ribbon

Smaller in size, it features a rubber strap and a steel or yellow-gold case. The rubber strap allows more sport-related use of the Première watch, which in this version is water-resistant up to 30m.

A watch designed and created for women instead of a scaled down version of a men's model.

Première Iconic Chain

A more discreet version of the Première Originale watch, available in steel only.

Première Gourmette

This is a more understated version of the Première, featuring a chain bracelet without leather interlacing and a metal cabochon.

Première Ceramic

Attached with a bracelet featuring metal and ceramic, the watch pays homage to the Première's sister model, the J12. The ceramic material was used for the first time in the J12 and makes this watch virtually scratch-proof.

Première Rock

A more youthful version of the Première watch thanks to its double-wrap bracelet for a more casual look.

ICONIC ITERATIONS

The Première collection has been expanded into bags, jewellery and objects for the home, all inspired by the famous watch.

Première Watch Minaudière

In 2015, Karl Lagerfeld paid tribute to the Première watch in the 'Paris Dubai' collection. A piece highly coveted by connoisseurs of the fashion house, this rigid bag replicates the shape of the watch case. A long chain allows crossbody wear.

Première travel clock

Released in the 1990s, the clock was created to adorn bedside tables. It is easily transportable thanks to the folding design. The watch bracelet is replaced by a tassel attached to the case.

THE MADEMOISELLE AND THE J12

Following the release of the Première watch in the 1980s, other timepieces were created at Chanel, such as the Matelassé watch with a dial paying homage to the Classic Flap bag, and the Mademoiselle model. Both of these timepieces, however, were considered to be fashion watches. It was only at the beginning of the new millennium and after several years of research that Chanel unveiled its iconic J12, which elevated the fashion house to the rank of serious luxury watchmaker.

MATELASSÉ AND MADEMOISELLE

In the 1990s, various watch models were presented to the public by Chanel, in addition to the existing quartz models.

In 1990, three years after the launch of the Première, the Mademoiselle watch was released in a classic version in leather or steel, but also in a bracelet variant consisting of five rows of pearls. The latter was the most iconic of the Mademoiselle iterations. This was followed by the Chanel Matelassé watch, which celebrated the quilted motif of the 2.55 handbag.

MATELASSÉ

Dial with quilted finish, no numerals

Crown set with an onyx cabochon

Gold or steel case with the brand signature

Bracelet/strap in quilted leather, smooth leather, exotic leather or steel

Clasp in gold or steel

MADEMOISELLE

Simple, unadorned case in Art Deco style

Crown set with an onyx cabochon

Dial with Roman numerals set around a circle

Case in steel or gold

Bracelet/strap in steel, gold, pearls or leather

THE J12

The Chanel J12 watch was unveiled to the public in the year 2000. Designed by Jacques Helleu 'as a watch he would wear himself', this avant-garde piece was bound to make waves as soon as it was released. Intensely black and made of ceramic, it shook up the design codes of luxury watches at the time.

The iconic J12 elevated Chanel to the rank of serious luxury watchmaker.

Thanks to diamond powder polishing and the inclusion of titanium in the minerals used to make its components, the ceramic employed to manufacture the J12 is virtually scratch-proof

Steel unidirectional bezel

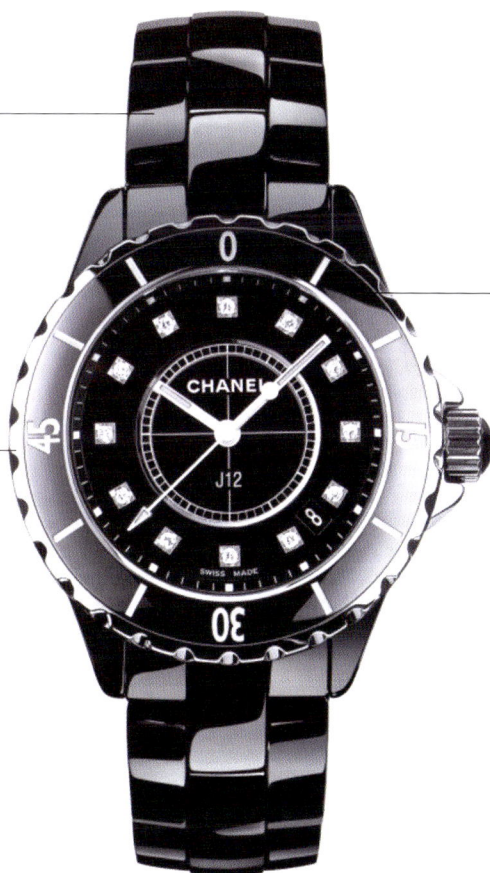

The screw-down crown guarantees water resistance at depths of up to 200m

Crown finished with a decorative black cabochon, a detail also found on the Première watch

A white variant of the J12 was launched in 2003, three years after the original black version was released.

THE J12 TODAY

The launch of the Première watch signalled Chanel's ambition to become a major player in the world of watchmaking. To be credible, the fashion house would need to have a presence in Switzerland, the birthplace of watchmaking know-how and since 1993 Chanel has owned the G&F Châtelain manufactured in La Chaux-de-Fonds, where its watches are made. The creation studio in Paris and the design office of the manufacturer in Switzerland work together to create new timepieces that consistently feature cutting-edge technology. Thanks to this acquisition, Chanel was able to develop its own watch movements for inclusion in its timepieces.

Before the year 2000, Chanel only made watches for women. But the sport-inspired and masculine feel of the J12 allowed it to expand its customer base. It was a risky wager for a fashion house with feminine roots but one that paid off. Twenty years later, the J12 continues to be a must-have piece in the Chanel catalogue, both in its classic version and multiple variations.

Although the flagship J12 is black and white, iterations have appeared using other colours such as the Marine version with its blue detailing and the grey Chromatic. The palette of the J12 was also expanded by inlaying precious and semi-precious stones, such as sapphire, incorporated into both the bezel and dial.

J12 Marine, rotating bezel, in blue steel. The traditional ceramic bracelet has been replaced with a rubber strap. Water-resistant up to 300m.

Unveiled in 2011, the J12 Chromatic was presented as a fusion of white and black, with a grey colour created using titanium-based ceramic.

In a change from the usual black and white, several limited editions of the J12 were launched in the 2000s, such as this example featuring a bezel set with pink sapphires.

Launched in 2005 with an even more sport-inspired look, the Superleggera in aluminium alloy is much lighter than the other models.

◂ J12 watch with white strap, 2003.

Blue spinel

Sword-shaped hands

Visible screw

THE SANTOS

BY CARTIER

The history of the Santos watch started with a meeting and a subsequent friendship between the Brazilian aviator Alberto Santos-Dumont and Louis Cartier at the beginning of the 20th century. Created in 1904, it was the first pilot watch designed to be worn on the wrist. With models for both women and men, this legendary watch is synonymous with timeless elegance. The Santos watch introduced highly innovative concepts for the time in terms of its shape, minimalism and the precision of its proportions.

A PILOT WATCH

Alberto Santos-Dumont was an aviation pioneer and told Louis Cartier about the challenges of checking a pocket watch mid-flight. This type of timepiece is attached to a chain and was worn by men in the inside pocket of a jacket. To read the time on his pocket watch, Santos-Dumont had to let go of the controls...something he wanted to avoid at all costs for reasons that are easy to imagine. To help his friend, Louis Cartier designed a watch that attached to his wrist with a strap, allowing him to keep his hands on the controls while checking the time.

A HIGH-SOCIETY PHENOMENON

Santos-Dumont fully embraced the solution devised by Cartier and wore the watch on his wrist at various Parisian social events, attracting the attention of the gentlemen around him. Although development of the watch started in 1904, it was not released by Louis Cartier until 1911, and was housed in a gold or platinum case on a leather strap.

A MAN'S WATCH

The Santos de Cartier watch was the first ever wristwatch made for men: until then, they had been designed exclusively for women.

ICONIC ITERATIONS

The original version of the Santos watch is very different from the one we know today, as over time the model evolved into a more sport-inspired version. The timepiece was also produced in other designs.

A MORE AFFORDABLE WATCH

The modern Santos was released only in 1978. In the 1970s and 1980s, Cartier radically changed its business strategy. The goal was to expand its offering by making high-quality but more affordable objects. This new policy opened the doors of luxury to a larger clientele who previously had no access to it. The new Cartier Santos therefore featured a steel body to guarantee an attractive price, with detailing in yellow gold to create a luxury feel. It is easily recognizable thanks to its iconic steel bracelet with visible gold screws and a buckle fitted with a hidden clasp.

GOLD AND STEEL – SIGNATURE OF THE BRAND

The two-tone steel-and-gold finish and more casual look made the new Santos easy to match with all kinds of day and eveningwear. The Santos was the first two-colour watch made by Cartier, but this gold–steel combination would be used in several later models such as the Panthère, Cougar and Ballon Bleu.

Baignoire

Cougar

Panthère

Ballon Bleu

A WATCH SYMBOLIC OF SUCCESS

The launch of the Santos was accompanied by a significant marketing campaign. On 20 October 1978, a spectacular evening was held at the Musée de l'Air at Le Bourget aerodrome (an airport near Paris used for private jets and business flights) to unveil this new icon by Cartier, with many notable personalities in attendance. The Cartier Santos was quickly adopted by the international jet set.

In 1987, Michael Douglas wore an all-gold model in the film *Wall Street*, further increasing its desirability, with the model now seen as a symbol of social success. The Santos proved so popular that it inspired a collection of other everyday objects. The visible screws are the iconic signature of a product line that includes cufflinks, necklaces and sunglasses.

Santos watch in gold and steel, created in the 1980s.

Sunglasses from the Santos de Cartier line.

THE MUST

BY CARTIER

The 1970s were a critical decade for the House of Cartier and resulted in a complete change of strategy. After the events of May 1968, consumer habits changed rapidly, and the brand was forced to reinvent itself to reach a new clientele.

THE CARTIER REVOLUTION

During this period, the introduction of quartz watches created a crisis situation for luxury watchmaking. Former antique dealer Alain-Dominique Perrin was appointed managing director of the company in 1970 and decided to redefine and modernize the concept of luxury, while also making high-end products accessible to a wider audience. He started his quiet revolution with the humble lighter. The Must de Cartier lighter was released in 1973. It was so successful that other products followed in the same line: sunglasses, jewellery, desk clocks, pens and even a burgundy leather golf bag sporting the signature features of the line.

Must de Cartier glasses

Must de Cartier clutch bag

THE TANK WATCH

Released in 1977, this timepiece was made from neither gold nor platinum but silver-gilt (vermeil). This clever move combined one high-end metal with another to create a touch of luxury at an affordable price – a requirement of the Must line. Initially fitted with a mechanical movement and manual winding, the watches in the collection quickly switched to a quartz movement to stay in line with the latest market trends.

The case of the Tank was square, staying faithful to the original design. Various iterations were released in different designs and colours, featuring lacquered dials with or without numerals in burgundy, black or blue, and even three-colour combinations evoking the aesthetics of the Trinity ring.

Watch from the Tank Must de Cartier collection.

Watch from the Tank Must de Cartier collection in sliver-gilt with blue lacquered dial.

REVISITING A CLASSIC MODEL

With such a wide range of models and colours on offer, the Tank Must de Cartier quickly attracted loyal fans and became a best-seller for the brand until it was discontinued in the 1990s. The mark made by the model was so strong, however, that Cartier relaunched the Tank in 2021 with a quartz movement in a steel case.

ICONIC ITERATIONS

Following the success of the Tank watch, the brand quickly released other models under the Must line.

The **Must Vendôme**, with its circular, virtually uninterrupted case replicates the simplest watch shape. Connected to the case by slim horizontal metal bars, the strap floats elegantly on either side of the watch. And, of course, the Vendôme religiously observed Cartier design codes with a railway-track minute design, blue hands, and a winding crown decorated with a sapphire cabochon.

The Cartier signature is inscribed on the caseback.

Must Colisée, with a round domed case.

Vendôme Must Trinity version, with a three-gold dial.

Must Ronde, which has a thicker case than its sister model, the Vendôme.

Must Trinity with a circular cushioned swirl case, evoking the shape of the iconic Cartier ring.

The final timepiece released under the Must line was the **Cartier 21**. With a highly modern and sports-inspired look, this piece offers unrivalled originality in the world of watchmaking. Instead of appearing on the dial, the numerals are engraved on the case.

Unlike all other watches in the Must line, it was not sold in silver or silver-gilt, but made from steel with gold inlay. The bracelet is available in steel and gold or a leather version.

THE OYSTER

BY ROLEX

With its precision, water resistance and elegance, Rolex has become the world's best selling luxury watch brand, largely due to its breathtaking technological advances and the founder's obsession with excellence.

A NEW STYLE OF WATCH

In 1905, at the age of 24, German businessman Hans Wilsdorf founded a watchmaking company in London, with the production side of the business located in Switzerland. His aim was to replace the pocket watch with the wristwatch, as the former did not offer the versatility required by the new lifestyles of the emerging century and the rise in sport and leisure activities.

The challenges were significant: he needed not only to make the wristwatch robust but also, most importantly, to reduce the size of the mechanisms while maximizing the reliability of the parts. Registered as a brand name in 1908, Rolex obtained multiple patents from prestigious technical inspection bodies over the subsequent years, thanks to the perseverance of Wilsdorf.

In 1914, the designer even obtained the first 'Class A' certificate ever awarded to a wristwatch, meaning that its accuracy was on a par with that of navy chronometers.

MAJOR TECHNICAL CHALLENGES

At the beginning of the 20th century, wristwatches started to play an increasingly important role in the active and sporting lives of their owners. The Oyster watch is the result of a determined commitment to solving a new problem: that of water resistance, which would then allow watches to be worn in all circumstances. Prior to this, humidity and impurities could get under the dial of watches via the crown, resulting in damage to the movement. The persistence of Wilsdorf resulted in his teams developing a hermetically sealed system in 1926. It featured a screw-down crown to prevent infiltration into the mechanism.

This new watch, designed to be worn in water, was baptized the Oyster. Wilsdorf said of the name, 'Like an oyster, it can remain an unlimited time under water without detriment to its parts.'

WATERPROOF MARVEL

To prove its effectiveness, Rolex equipped a young English swimmer named Mercedes Gleitze with the Oyster watch during her crossing of the Channel in 1927. After the ten-hour ordeal, the watch emerged intact and perfectly functional. The Oyster watch was later displayed immersed in an aquarium in watchmakers' windows: irrefutable proof of its capabilities and a publicity stunt that has contributed to the Rolex myth ever since.

The Oyster made its mark on the world of watchmaking thanks to its innovative technology, and Rolex did not stop there: from 1931, the company filed a series of patents for an automatic winding mechanism featuring a freely swinging rotor. Known as the 'Perpetual' rotor, the mechanism would be adopted as a watchmaking industry standard. Watches with this type of rotor are self-winding thanks to the movement of the wearer's wrist, meaning that no manual action is required to keep it in working order. In addition to eliminating the effort of winding, the crown does not have to be moved back and forth, which can cause premature wear of the watch seals and make the case prone to water ingress.

The Rolex Oyster Perpetual is distinguished by a sophisticated mechanism that allows self-winding through the movement of the wrist. The Oyster watch is fully water-resistant.

Rolex Oyster Submariner case for the Compagnie Maritime d'Expertise, or COMEX, a commercial diving company.

The Rolex logo is a five-pointed crown symbolizing victory, prestige and perfectionism. The gold colour represents the rich traditions of the founder and his watchmaking excellence.

'Simplicity is a difficult art.'

Thierry Stern

THE BADGE OF SPANISH KNIGHTS

Calatrava was taken from the name of a 12th-century order of Spanish knights. Its insignia combined the shape of a Greek cross with four fleurs-de-lys. It was adopted as the Patek Philippe logo in 1887.

Calatrava in yellow gold with a guilloched 'Clous de Paris' bezel and a date window at three o'clock. The first model was released in 1934. A hobnail pattern forms small pyramids on the bezel. Today, the line is making a strong comeback with a new, highly contemporary version available in rose gold or white gold, and powered by a brand-new hand-wound Patek Philippe movement with a 65-hour power reserve.

Dial with Calatrava cross motif.

Calatrava created in 1990, with dual time zone. This model is extremely rare today.

THE CALATRAVA

BY PATEK PHILIPPE

Refined and discreet thanks to its pure lines, the Calatrava is probably one of the most elegant watches of the 20th century. Ironically, it has become an icon of the watch brand, even though its understated, classic appearance is in sharp contrast to the chronographs and complication pocket watches that the Swiss company has specialized in and won numerous awards for since the end of the 19th century.

THE MASTER OF UNDERSTATEMENT

The first Calatrava watch was released in 1932 under the name Ref 96 and was given its current name only in the 1980s. The first movement of the timepiece was designed by LeCoultre, as was the case for other luxury watches of the period. A few years later, Patek Philippe developed its own in-house movement for the timepiece.

Simple in appearance, the case of the Calatrava watch is inspired by the Bauhaus design movement, which existed from 1919 to 1933 and promoted the idea that form should follow function. The sleek, minimalist aesthetic of the Calatrava has withstood the test of time with ease. It has established itself as the quintessential round wristwatch and as one of the most beautiful symbols of Patek Philippe style. The ultimate in elegance, it has captivated multiple generations thanks to its timeless perfection and superbly understated look.

A WATCH MADE TO BE TIMELESS

Patek Philippe embraces the concept of longevity, as evidenced by the brand's famous marketing strapline: 'You never actually own a Patek Philippe. You merely look after it for the next generation.'

Today, the Calatrava continues to be one of the flagship models of the watchmaking house, with more than 13 variations available, all made from precious metals (yellow gold, white gold and platinum).

THE CAPE COD

The Cape Cod watch was the fruit of a long haul flight from the Hermès offices in Paris to the East Coast of the United States. While on holiday in Cape Cod with his French-American wife, Henri d'Origny, creative director at Hermès, drew his inspiration for the watch from this Massachusetts peninsula, a favoured destination of the jet set. The watch was released in 1991 and is now a must-have piece by the famous fashion house.

A HERMÈS SQUARE IN A RECTANGLE

When Jean-Louis Dumas, the CEO of Hermès, asked Henri d'Origny to design a square watch, the creative director demonstrated both obedience and defiance in carrying out the task. He started with a slightly rounded square and surrounded it with two Chaîne d'ancre (anchor chain) half links at the top and bottom. The outcome was definitely a square watch, although set within a rectangle!

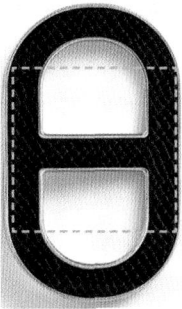

THE GOLDEN AGE OF THE 1990S

Although the Cape Cod watch was an immediate success on its release in 1991, its finest hour came in 1998 when Martin Margiela took over as creative director of the fashion house. He had the simple but brilliant idea of giving it a very long strap, which could easily be doubled around the wrist. This was made from Barenia leather, a smooth natural calfskin that develops a wonderful patina over time. Moreover, the sublime caramel colour was equally appealing to both women and men.

Martin Margiela was the first designer to impart such strength and elegance to a time-piece. The fact that the Cape Cod strap is interchangeable has also greatly contributed to the success of the watch. A simple mechanism allows the strap to be easily removed and replaced with another to match the wearer's outfit or mood.

ICONIC ITERATIONS

Cape Cod Automatique
The double-wrap strap was regularly featured in advertising and catalogues, and became one of the symbols of the Margiela period at Hermès.

◄ Hermès Cape Cod automatic watch in steel with white double-wrap strap.

Cape Cod in yellow gold
set with diamonds.

Cape Cod Nantucket in steel
The Cape Cod Nantucket features a narrower case. Its name derives from a small island 48km south of the Cape Cod peninsula.

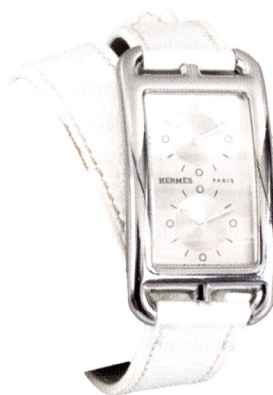

Cape Cod Tonneau
Several iterations were released in the 2000s and 2010s, including the Cape Cod Tonneau with its delicately curved case.

Available today in several different sizes and materials, the Cape Cod watch continues to be a must-have signature timepiece by Hermès.

A CINEMATIC ICON?
In Pedro Almodóvar's 2016 film *Julieta*, the title
character played by Adriana Ugarte wore the
Hermès Heure H watch.

THE HEURE H

With a case in the shape of the initial letter of the fashion house, the Heure H watch is the most identifiable timepiece from Hermès. While the iconic H had already been used in several designs, such as the Évelyne bag and the famous Hermès belt, this was the first time that it featured on the wrist, resulting in a must-have accessory highly valued by all connoisseurs of the brand.

THE H CASE

One of the great designers of the Hermès fashion house, Philippe Mouquet was responsible for this concept of lettered time. Since the 1980s, the former applied arts student – recruited by Hermès after winning two awards in a row in young designer competitions – has injected his playful imagination into everything he touches: leather goods, gold and silver jewellery, prints, perfume bottles and more. So when the moment came for his first watch design, his confidence and exuberance once again came into play when framing the passing of time. His masterstroke was to make a case from the signature H of the fashion house.

THE STRENGTH OF A LOGO

Released in 1996, this was the first Hermès watch with an obvious logo, and a departure from the fashion house's usual design codes of discreet luxury. And, like other time-pieces, its commercial strength would lie in the wide choice of colours available for its straps and dials. In just a few months, the logo timepiece was a best-seller and would eventually become a classic.

The Heure H quickly became the icon of a generation of watches that had luxury credentials but were also accessible to a wide audience. And its colour and shape meant that it could be worn by both men and women.

It was the first Hermès watch with an obvious logo, and a departure from the fashion house's usual design codes of discreet luxury.

Caramel strap

Other shades were also available, such as grey and black. To add a more luxurious feel to this sport-inspired piece, Hermès designed other models in gold or steel, or with a diamond-set dial and case.

H-shaped case

Still available in the Hermès catalogue, the watch comes in four different sizes:
· Mini (21mm)
· Small (25mm)
· Medium (30mm)
· Large (34mm).

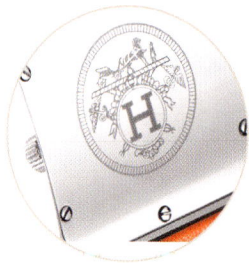

The Hermès logo on the back of the case.

An iconic variation, the Heure H watch in a round design in steel.

THE REVERSO

What happens when a watch meets the equestrian sport of polo?
As unlikely as it seems, such an encounter resulted in one of the
icons of modern watchmaking.

MANUFACTURING AS A FORM OF CHALLENGE

The year was 1931. After a polo match, a British officer showed the broken glass of his watch to César de Trey, a retailer of luxury watches. The officer challenged him to come up with a watch that could withstand the rigours of a polo match. Willingly accepting the challenge, de Trey turned to Jacques-David LeCoultre, a manufacturer of watch and clock movements, who in turn contacted his partner, the Parisian watchmaker Edmond Jaeger.

A TECHNICAL DESIGN FEAT

Edmond Jaeger entrusted the mission to engineer René-Alfred Chauvot. Chauvot set about designing the case and, on 4 March 1931, filed a patent for a 'watch capable of sliding in its chassis and flipping over'. This sliding system meant that the watch crystal was protected from knocks and accidents.

BIRTH OF A WATCHMAKING HOUSE

At the beginning of the 1930s, the Jaeger-LeCoultre brand did not yet exist. The two companies were independent but had been partners since 1903. It was only in 1937, after years of collaboration, that they decided to merge and become the brand of Jaeger-LeCoultre, today owned by the Swiss Richemont luxury goods group.

AN ART DECO WATCH

Designed during the Art Deco period, the case of the Reverso watch reflects the aesthetics of the time, with its horizontal gadroon decoration and simple, geometric lines.

In principle, the only purpose of flipping the watch over to make the back visible was to protect the dial, but this feature would play a significant role in the success of the Reverso. It allowed the owner to personalize and discreetly decorate the timepiece with engravings, inscriptions and even lacquered patterns. These secrets remained hidden and were only displayed at the owner's discretion when they chose to flip the case over.

ICONIC ITERATIONS

The Reverso was so successful that other luxury houses released their own models in which the case of the watch could be turned over to protect the crystal – for example, the Cartier Basculante, created in 1932.

More than sixty years after its release, a major variation of the Reverso was issued in 1994. Known as the Reverso Duoface, this model featured a dual time zone. It was followed in 1997 by the Reverso Duetto, a women's version with a double dial.

Limited-edition Reverso Duetto with dual time zone and line of diamonds.

Reverso Duetto watch.

Today, more than fifty versions of the Reverso watch are available in the Jaeger-LeCoultre catalogue for both men and women.

THE SERPENTI

BY BVLGARI

Italian in origin but now belonging to the LVMH group, Bvlgari was founded in Rome in 1884 by Greek silversmith Sotírios Voúlgaris (Sotirio Bulgari in Italian). It is probably the most famous jewellery house in the world thanks to its collections, which combine colour and volume to create extraordinary pieces.

A WATCH OR A JEWEL?

In 1948, when the Serpenti watch was released, it was described as a 'jewellery watch' to be wrapped around the wrist. But the Serpenti has evolved so much over the decades that it could now be considered a standalone piece of jewellery in its own right.

THE BVLGARI SERPENT

The name Serpenti comes from the Italian for 'serpents' or 'snakes'. This shape is so intimately linked with Bvlgari today that it could be seen as part of the brand's DNA. The symbolism of the serpent is enormously important to this luxury brand, and in 2016 Bvlgari sponsored an exhibition in Rome exclusively dedicated to the snake in art, as depicted in sculptures, paintings, costumes and jewellery.

The brand's choice of the serpent, a mysterious and captivating animal with a sinuous and enveloping shape, was not made randomly. In mythology, the snake's ability to regenerate and perpetually change its skin has made it a symbol of immortality. Throughout its history, Bvlgari has continuously reinvented the Serpenti, showcasing its eternal magnetism with each new creation.

A bracelet wrapped multiple times around the wrist is a feature not only of the Serpenti watch but also several other Bvlgari creations.

SERPENTI WITH SCALES

In the models from the 1940s and 1950s, the body of the snake acted as a bracelet and was produced using the Tubogas technique, in which metal strips are wrapped around a core. This made the design flexible enough to be wrapped around the wrist.

Over time, the body of the snake would evolve to become more realistic. Precious metals were used to replicate the scales of a snake's body. These were enamelled in different shades to broaden the colour palette of the watch.

THE ICON ELIZABETH TAYLOR

Elizabeth Taylor was the great ambassador of the Serpenti, and of Bvlgari. She also owned several pieces from the collection. In 1962, she appeared in Joseph L. Mankiewicz's film *Cleopatra* wearing a gold-and-platinum Serpenti with a diamond-set head and tail. In 2011, the jewel was sold at auction in New York for $974,500 (£609,000).

The Tubogas technique gives the Serpenti great flexibility.

Serpenti flexible ring in gold and steel with diamond-set head and tail.

ICONIC ITERATIONS

Today, two models are available in the Bvlgari catalogue: a Serpenti with a Tubogas springband body in the brand's permanent collections, and a Serpenti with enamelled scales in its high jewellery collections.

In the 2000s, the snake was also adopted as the symbol of Bvlgari leather goods. It is the star of the Serpenti Forever accessories collection, which includes iconic bags, costume jewellery, wallets and other small leather goods in different styles, colours and materials, expressing all the talent of the great Roman jewellery house.

Bvlgari Serpenti created in the 2000s, with a Tubogas springband body.

Bag from the Serpenti Forever collection, in brown leather with snake's head clasp.

In 2021, a new variation of the Serpenti line was released. Serpenti Viper is a more minimalist, geometric collection adapted to a new generation of customers.

LE/ MERVEILLE/
DE BABELLOU

Interview with Isabelle Klein

How did you come up with the idea of setting up a shop?

As far back as I can remember, I've always been fascinated by objects from the past. I was born in the countryside in southern France, surrounded by vineyards, and I was lucky enough to have a very well-turned-out mother who loved fashion and an aunt whom I deeply admired, a brilliant seamstress. I owe a lot to both of them. I was immersed in a very creative world where I was taught about beauty, refinement, elegance and femininity very early on. I developed a taste for beautiful materials and beautiful things. I learned all the different sewing techniques. Everything amazed me, and I had an obvious taste for eccentricity.

I remember my first purchase as if it were yesterday. It was one summer at a flea market stall. I stopped in my tracks, completely fascinated, in front of a long, black 1920s dress covered from head to toe in bead embroidery. The dress was heavy, very heavy. At least 5kg of beads on such fine silk! It was stunning, love at first sight! The lady was asking 500 francs for the dress. That was the amount I'd earned from helping my father. I didn't hesitate for a single second: I bought the dress and walked off with it like a trophy. I folded it up and put it in a box in tissue paper. I never wore the dress; I was too afraid of damaging it, thinking the fabric might tear or the beads would fall off. But it was my treasure, bought with the sweat of my brow. That was undoubtedly the day that my true passion for vintage fashion began.

In 2007, after many years as a second-hand goods dealer and flea market trader, an idea came to me: to open a new concept, a vintage fashion store that would recreate the atmosphere of a fashion boutique from the 1950s. I wanted to devise a store design that would bring out the very best in the pieces on sale. I used mirrors, counters, dressing tables and old display cases to reinvent and recreate an atmosphere of yesteryear.

What makes your shop special?

I opened my first fashion boutique in October 2008 at the Paul Bert market, Saint-Ouen, in the northern suburbs of Paris. It was immediately successful. My concept is an innovative one. What makes me happiest is helping my visitors to dream, and giving them a sense of romance and emotion. But after a year, it was time to have a rethink. My customers were continuously asking me for big brands and big designer labels. It was obvious that I absolutely had to expand my offering and bring in designer pieces and more high-end products. I started to offer a wider selection of major brands from the 1940s to the 2000s, such as Chanel, Dior, Yves Saint Laurent, Paco Rabanne, Valentino, Hermès, Givenchy, Balmain, Loris Azzaro, John Galliano, Lanvin, Louis Féraud, Jean-Louis Scherrer, Nina Ricci, Thierry Mugler, Jean Paul Gaultier, Christian Lacroix, Versace, Goyard, Louis Vuitton and many more.

My boutique now sells a vast selection of exceptional products: bags, jewellery, evening dresses, hats, accessories and scarves. It's impossible to leave without falling for something. My store is like a sanctuary and contains lounge areas, encouraging partners and friends to relax while they're waiting. All the pieces are cleaned (using a luxury eco-friendly dry-cleaning process), and restored if necessary, in accordance with professional practices. We are open at the weekend but also receive private appointments on weekdays.

'I'm constantly looking for the rare pearl, the impossible-to-find, the exceptional piece.'

Who are your customers?

My clientele is international (American, Asian and European): the whole world comes to the flea market. These customers like really beautiful ready-to-wear pieces, but are most interested in haute couture. The demand for rare and unique pieces is growing, as is the interest in them. Chanel and Dior are all the rage. Every woman in the world wants to have her own Chanel jacket, bag or necklace, or her own Kelly or Birkin bag by Hermès. The craze for vintage luxury fashion is here to stay. Many celebrities have come to the boutique and continue to visit us regularly, such as, to name a few, Salma Hayek, Florent Pagny, Mick Jagger, Eva Green, Demi Moore, Lily Collins, Whoopi Goldberg, Amal Clooney, Valérie Lemercier, Clémentine Célarié, Kendall Jenner, Cristina Cordula, Gwyneth Paltrow, Maria Grazia Chiuri, John Galliano, Jeremy Scott and Jacquemus. It was Amal Clooney who gave me the best compliment. She congratulated me, saying that I had the most beautiful vintage fashion store in the world.

What is the rarest piece you have sold?

I've never tired of doing this job over all these years, and the passion is still there. I'm constantly looking for the rare pearl, the impossible-to-find, the exceptional piece. I remember the fully embroidered and beaded Christian Lacroix haute couture corset worn by Beyoncé (a real museum piece). And I fell in love with an incredible top from the House of Chanel covered in jewel crosses, 63 in total, and worn to close the Pre-Autumn 2008 runway show.

LES MERVEILLES DE BABELLOU
Marché Paul Bert
93400 Saint-Ouen-sur-Seine
lesmerveillesdebabellou.com
Instagram: @lesmerveillesdebabellou

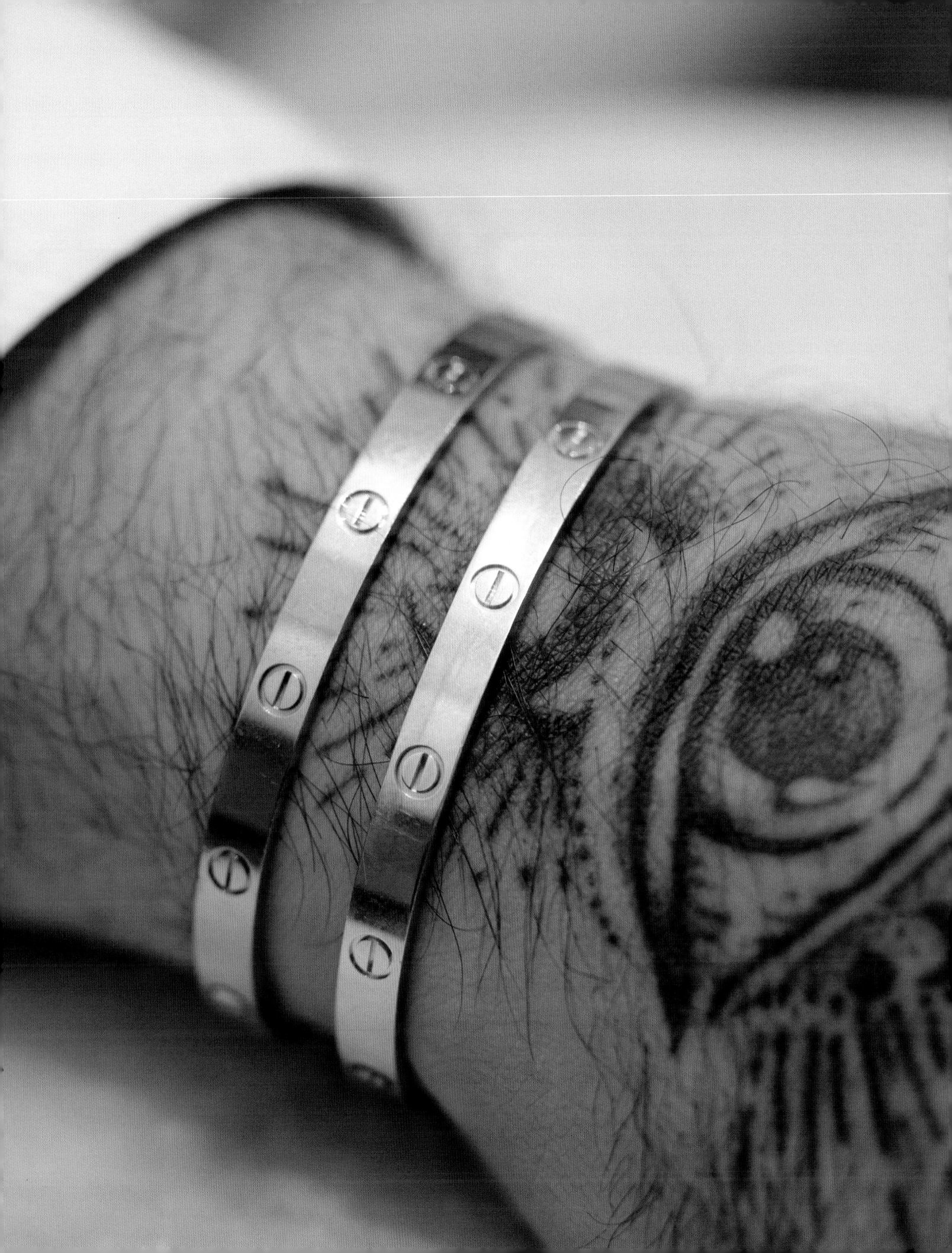

THE LOVE BRACELET

BY CARTIER

When a bracelet is called 'Love', the first image that comes to mind is a piece of jewellery in the shape of a heart, the international symbol of romantic emotions, and a constant presence thanks to today's use of emojis. But here there are no hearts or other superfluous ornaments to embody the concept. Instead, Cartier has deliberately flown in the face of such clichés with this timeless, industrial-looking design.

A FAMILY STORY

The story began in 1847 when Louis-François Cartier took over the workshop of Adolphe Picard at 29 rue Montorgueil, Paris. His son Alfred joined the family business in 1859, the year the Cartier store moved to 9 boulevard des Italiens. In just over a decade, the small Parisian workshop successfully attracted the attention of a renowned clientele and rose to the ranks of an established jewellers.

The year 1898 was a turning point: Alfred decided to involve his eldest son, Louis, in the business, which he himself had inherited from his father. The House of Cartier was already a recognized institution when Alfred left the boulevard des Italiens and moved the company to rue de la Paix, near the celebrated place Vendôme. Louis Cartier was only 23 years old at the time. His two brothers, Pierre and Jacques, were still too young to be directly involved in the family business. Eventually, under the patronage of the three jeweller brothers who were raised surrounded by the traditions of the profession, Cartier would grow as never before...

NON-GENDERED SIMPLICITY

The story of the Love bracelet began in 1969 in New York, with a key figure in the history of Cartier: Aldo Cipullo. A designer of Italian origin, he joined Cartier in the 1960s after a stint at Tiffany & Co. His bracelet design immediately stood out with its simple, innovative, timeless and unisex aesthetic.

The characteristics of the Love bracelet have allowed it to weather multiple decades without losing any of its appeal, as is the case for another iconic creation by Cipullo for Cartier, the Juste un clou bracelet.

The Love bracelet is the only piece in the luxury house to have not only the Cartier signature but also that of Aldo Cipullo engraved on the inside, demonstrating the unprecedented influence of the Italian-born designer.

A VERY SPECIAL CLASP

The Love bracelet features the sleekest of lines: a bangle bracelet consisting of a rigid and uniform ring, it sits elegantly on the wrist and is decorated with screws around the whole outer circumference. But behind its simple appearance, this unique piece actually hides something revolutionary in its closure system. Shunning the design of classic jewellery clasps, the bracelet is closed using a silver-gilt screwdriver supplied for the task. This operation definitely requires someone else to assist, but it means that the join line of the clasp is completely invisible once the bracelet is closed!

In some ways, this process evokes the symbolism of the medieval chastity belt, which brings us back to the name of the bracelet. It takes two people to attach it, the idea being that the wearer's loved one performs the operation and keeps the screwdriver. Once the bracelet is closed, it cannot be removed by sliding it over the hand like a traditional bangle: it encircles the wrist for ever, symbolizing eternal love.

AN AFFORDABLE PIECE OF CARTIER JEWELLERY?
The Love bracelet was priced at $250 (roughly £105) when it was released in New York in 1969.

A MODEL FOR ALL ETERNITY

As soon as it launched, the jet set from all over the world, and especially New York, enthusiastically adopted the Love bracelet, and it was seen on the wrists of many famous couples. One of its first ambassadors was the actor Elizabeth Taylor: Cartier gifted her a pair of bracelets, one for her and the other for her husband Richard Burton. Paradoxically, although their love story was neither ideal nor eternal, their endorsement greatly contributed to the success of the legendary piece.

Although it has undergone some minor modifications, the Love bracelet sold today remains largely faithful to the original model designed by Aldo Cipullo, and is available in various versions, with the screw motif continuing to be the common thread of the collection.

ICONIC ITERATIONS

Pair of Love hoop earrings in yellow gold.
In the inlaid versions, the screws disappear to make way for precious stones.

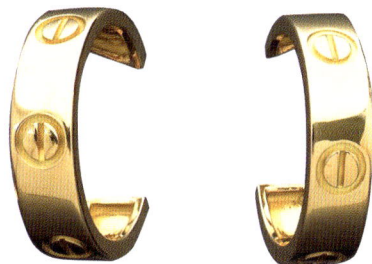

Love ring featuring the same motifs and an identical closure system.

Today, the Love bracelet is also available in an open bangle version, which no longer requires a screwdriver or another person to close it.

JUSTE UN CLOU

BY CARTIER

The Juste un clou (Just a Nail) bracelet is a rebellious piece that disrupted the design codes of conventional jewellery. A far cry from classic sources of inspiration, such as flowers, animals and other decorative objects, it glorifies the nail, an everyday, utilitarian and even humdrum object, by transforming it into a piece of jewellery presented in a luxury case.

A BRACELET INITIALLY UNNOTICED...

Now a flagship and iconic Cartier piece, when the bracelet was first launched it failed to emulate the dazzling heights of the Love model. It was only when it was reissued in 2012 that it became a worldwide best-seller. Aldo Cipullo created the Clou (its original name) in 1971, drawing his inspiration from a small item of hardware to create a playful design. He was also paying discreet homage to such Surrealist artists as Marcel Duchamp who diverted common objects from their intended use to make works of art. No doubt because the bracelet was way ahead of its time, sales were so disappointing that production was eventually discontinued in the 1980s. And so it lay dormant in the Cartier archives, along with other designs waiting for their day.

THE ART OF SMALL THINGS

The bracelet was relaunched in 2012 and renamed Juste un clou to mark the occasion. This time around, its modern and playful looks proved to be a huge hit. Like all best-sellers, it was available in varying degrees of luxury. Today, the Juste un clou line includes more than 90 products. Building on this success, Cartier expanded its 'hardware' line in 2017. Luxury DIYers could now add the Écrou (Nut) bracelet to their toolbox. More than any other jeweller, Cartier has been able to transform the 'little things', often ignored or even looked down on by society, into objects of desire.

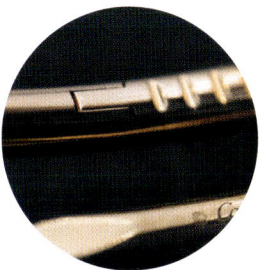

The technicality of the bracelet lies in its closure system, which is hidden in the head of the nail. The mechanism is invisible and undetectable when the bracelet is worn.

TRINITY

BY CARTIER

An icon of the House of Cartier, the Trinity ring is a hundred years old. But this grande dame has lost none of her power or her magnificence. The ring was, is and will continue to be one of the iconic pieces of jewellery of the 20th and 21st centuries.

THREE GOLDS

The first ring with three interlocking bands was created in 1924. It was quickly followed by a matching bracelet. Contrary to popular belief, the Trinity is not named after the three golds used to make it: yellow, rose and white. In fact, the rings were originally made from platinum and just two types of gold, without the use of gemstones.

BIRTH OF A RING FOR SATURN

What do the three bands mean? Opinions on the subject are divided. According to the most popular theory, the bands symbolize love, friendship and fidelity. But others believe that they represent the past, present and future. As is often the case, the truth is more prosaic. Louis Cartier, the designer of the ring, was not intending to create an object full of symbolic meaning, but instead wanted to satisfy the desires of his friend and client, Jean Cocteau, who had asked for a 'triply Saturnian ring'. Cocteau loved the ring so much that he wore two on his little finger, helping to create a legend that would be adopted and magnified by couples around the world.

ELEGANCE AND DREAMS

The simplicity and elegance of the piece made it popular with both women and men of all generations. Its enormous success was also due to the fact that it was commonly chosen to mark important life events such as engagements and weddings. Like many Cartier creations, the Trinity was eventually issued in a Must de Cartier version, available in a multitude of different designs.

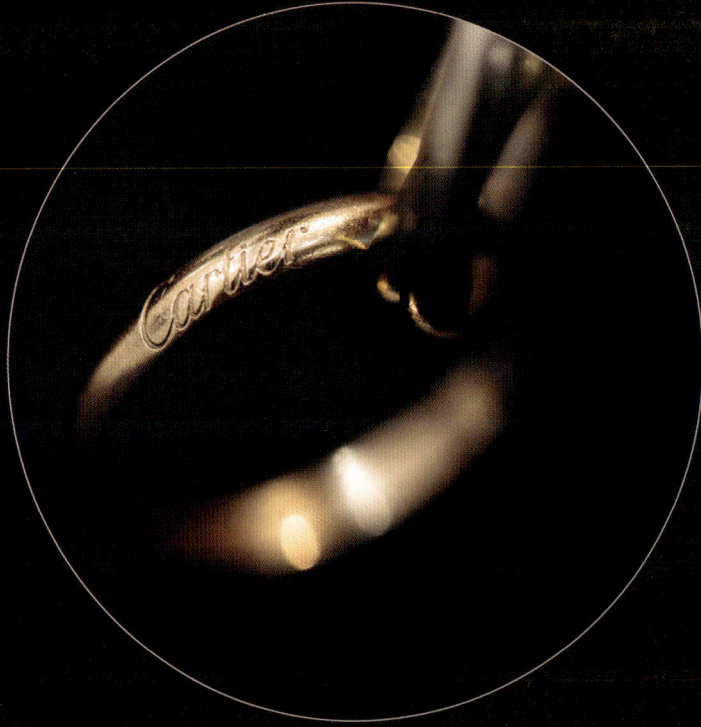

CARTIER SIGNATURE
The size and serial number are engraved
on the inside of one of the rings.

ICONIC ITERATIONS

Today, Trinity is not just a ring but a complete product line in the Cartier catalogue. It includes earrings, necklaces and bracelets, as well as bags decorated with the three rings. In 2024, Cartier launched a new design featuring a Trinity with square bands.

Trinity ring, Must de Cartier collection.

Trinity bracelet.

Trinity earrings in white, rose and yellow gold.

Trinity ring with pavé-set diamonds.

Trinity fountain pen, Must de Cartier collection.

THE MENOTTE/ BRACELET

BY DINH VAN

The Parisian jewellery house Dinh Van was founded in 1965 by Jean Dinh Van, a former artisan at Cartier of French-Vietnamese heritage. The aim of his minimalist, geometric and unfussy designs was to showcase everyday objects and create practical and easy-to-wear jewellery.

The Menottes design worn as a necklace.

ENHANCING THE EVERYDAY

The inspiration drawn from everyday objects is particularly obvious in the star piece of the jewellery house: the Menottes bracelet. In fact, the model was incorrectly named, as it represents two interlocking key heads rather than handcuffs (*menottes* in French).

The design of this piece is interesting because, unusually, the major decorative elements (the two key heads) also function as the clasp. They interlock via grooves in the structure of each head, giving them the appearance of handcuffs. When it was created, this highly visible clasp went against the technical and aesthetic innovations of the 1970s. At that time, the trend was for hidden clasps, the ideal being even to make them disappear, as in the Cartier Love and Juste un clou bracelets.

DESIRABLE ITERATIONS

Designed for both men and women, the Menottes bracelet enjoyed great commercial success thanks to the multitude of variants produced. The Menottes and its derivatives were available in several sizes and materials, on cords or chains, and in gold or silver.

A staple of the Dinh Van brand, today's collection includes more than a hundred pieces of jewellery: bracelets, pendants and earrings to suit all budgets, with pieces ranging from a few hundred pounds or dollars for silver versions to several thousand for gold variants set with gemstones.

THE CHAÎNE D'ANCRE

BY HERMÈS

Starting out as a maker of harnesses and saddles, Hermès is traditionally associated with the equestrian world. However, one of the most recognizable collections of the luxury house is not linked to horses but the sea: the Chaîne d'ancre line.

NAUTICAL INSPIRATION

The origins of the Chaîne d'ancre bracelet date back to 1937. While strolling along the Normandy coast, Robert Dumas, son-in-law of Émile Hermès, was drawn to the anchor chains attached to boats he saw in the local harbour. He decided that a miniaturized version in precious metal would make a pretty bracelet. This resulted in a piece of jewellery with generous curves and interconnected silver links, reminiscent of an anchor forever chained to its boat. On 3 March 1938, he filed a patent for the bracelet, which featured large links and a toggle clasp made up of a ring and T-bar.

THE CHOICE OF SILVER

Originally designed in silver, the Chaîne d'ancre bracelet was problematic for Hermès because its manufacturers at the time only accepted orders in gold and platinum. Only the workshop of Gaétan de Percin, which had recently opened in 1938, agreed to make the bracelet in silver, initiating a long partnership that would result in the production of many other flagship models for the fashion house.

An iconic model made by Gaétan de Percin for Hermès, the Boucle sellier (Saddle Buckle) bracelet, created in the 1940s.

A TIMELESS MOTIF

Thanks to its robust and solid design, the Chaîne d'ancre bracelet can be passed down from generation to generation. The shape of the links has varied slightly over time. Originally straight, they are now slightly more rounded. Today, this unisex bracelet is available in five different link widths and worn in its various iterations by men and women of all ages. The Chaîne d'ancre has become a must-have and iconic piece of Hermès heritage. It has been reinterpreted for decades in many different designs by the fashion house, including bags, porcelain, ready-to-wear, shoes and hair accessories.

The body of the bracelet offers excellent resistance to wear and breakage thanks to its thick links.

The absence of a spring or other type of mechanism in the closure system eliminates the need for repairs.

The large T-bar (or toggle) of the clasp prevents the bracelet from opening accidentally.

THE CHAÎNE D'ANCRE:
AN ICONIC HERMÈS MOTIF

Chaîne d'ancre handbag
In *porosus* crocodile, created in 1960.

Hermès sandals
With anchor-chain pattern in multi-coloured leather, created in the 2020s.

In the Loop
Created in 2023, with handles in the shape of an anchor-chain link.

Chaîne d'ancre change tray in porcelain
Design by Philippe Mouquet, *c.*1990.

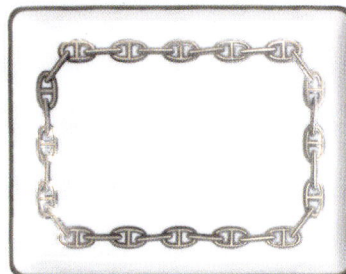

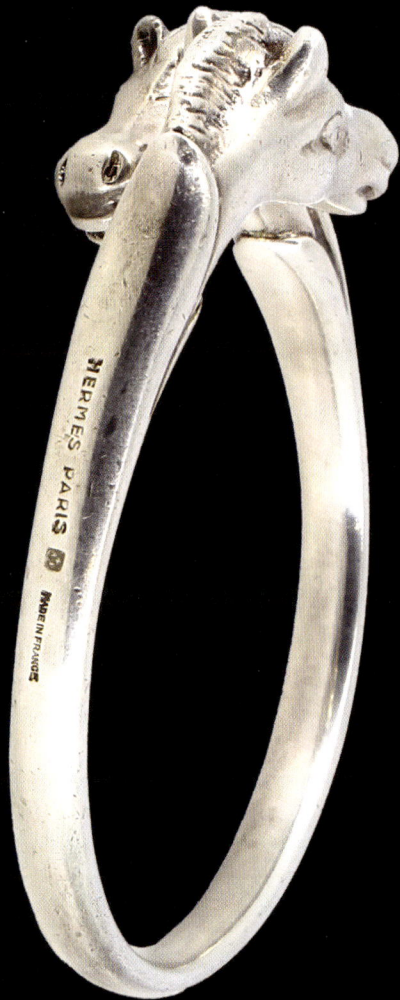

Vintage bracelet in solid silver with two horses' heads,
by Ravinet d'Enfert.

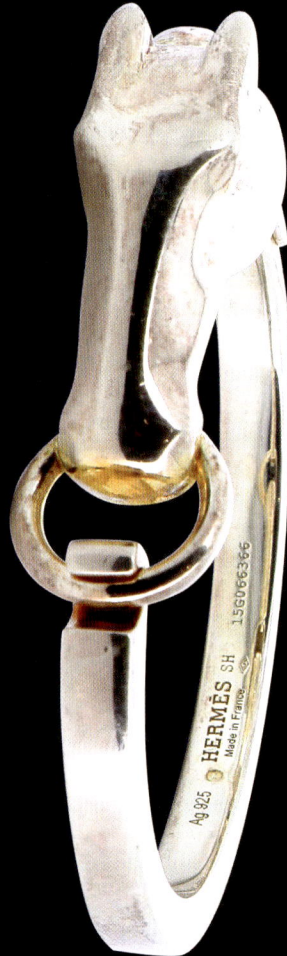

Modern bracelet reinterpreted
by Pierre Hardy.

THE EQUIDIA LINE

BY HERMÈS

Each prestigious label has a hidden army of artisans, experts and magicians of material who are constantly innovating and overcoming technical challenges to create ever-more-perfect pieces. This is particularly true at Hermès, which has always called on the services of the best makers in all categories. With its Parisian roots, Hermès naturally chose a specialist from the city for its jewellery and goldwork, the company Ravinet d'Enfert.

THE CORNERSTONE OF HERMÈS

Maison Ravinet d'Enfert was founded in 1891 by two partners, Louis Ravinet and Charles d'Enfert. It developed its own collections of decorative objects and tableware, and also collaborated with several luxury houses, including Hermès, for more than thirty years. Out of all the pieces created for Hermès (for the Balle de golf and Cordage lines), the line that has most successfully stood the test of time is undoubtedly Equidia which, as its name suggests, celebrates the head of the horse, the talismanic animal of Hermès.

JEWELLERY AND EVERYDAY OBJECTS

The Equidia line consisted of silver and silver-gilt jewellery, including a stunning bracelet depicting the overlapping heads of two horses nuzzling each other. A whole line of desk accessories was also produced in gold-plated and silver-plated metal: letter openers, pencil cases, magnifying glasses, change trays, letter clips and so on. Over the decades, the horse's head evolved and was depicted with different expressions, giving each object a unique character. Production was discontinued when Ravinet d'Enfert closed down in 1984.

COLLECTOR'S PIECES

Later on, Pierre Hardy, creative director of Hermès jewellery, paid homage to the Equidia line with the design of the Au galop jewellery line, featuring a refined and stylized horse's head. As the Equidia line was discontinued many years ago, these pieces are now highly sought after by collectors around the world, who appreciate their elegance and the precision with which they were made.

ICONIC ITERATIONS

Equidia bracelet in silver-gilt
In this single-head model, the Hermès signature is visible on the inside of the bracelet.

Au galop necklace in silver
With horse's head, designed by
Pierre Hardy.

Silver-plated letter clip, with Hermès stamp on the base.

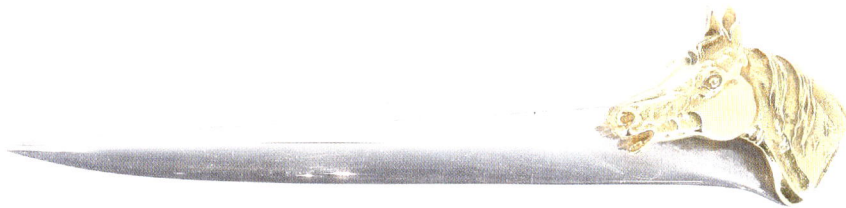

Silver-plated and gold-plated letter opener.

Silver-plated 'tastevin' wine-tasting cup.

Silver-plated desk magnifying glass.

The Chopard signature

HAPPY DIAMONDS

BY CHOPARD

Chopard, a Swiss watchmaking house founded in 1860, is today better known for its jewellery, thanks to the iconic Happy Diamonds collection, first created in its workshops in 1976.

FROM WATCHMAKING TO JEWELLERY

Chopard originally specialized in high-precision watchmaking, pocket watches and chronometers. In 1976, the company wanted to find a new way of setting diamonds in watches and developed a system that allowed them to float freely between two sapphire crystals on the dial.

This system was created by the brand's designer Ronald Kurowski: the diamonds were 'set' in white gold cubes with a bevelled base, making them look like little drops of water dancing freely between the two crystals. 'These diamonds are happier when they are free!' exclaimed Karin Scheufele, owner of the luxury house, when she first saw the collection. The name of the line, Happy Diamonds, was inspired by her words.

A RANGE OF PRECIOUS AND PLAYFUL JEWELLERY

This technique of inserting diamonds, rather than setting them, was used in watches for both men and women. Nearly a decade later, in 1985, the first piece of jewellery in the collection was created: a clown with moving limbs and head, a diamond-set bow tie, sapphire eyes and a ruby-set hat. The clown's torso contained Happy Diamonds and coloured gems that slid playfully around.

Other pieces in gold and diamonds would follow. Naive, joyful and fun, elephants, teddy bears and mice were all released by the brand, marking Chopard's growing importance in the world of jewellery.

'These diamonds are happier
when they are free!'
Karin Scheufele

AN ODE TO WOMEN

The Happy Diamonds line became an icon of bohemian and stylish luxury. It conveyed the freedom of women able to delight in their lives by constantly reinventing where they wanted to go and who they wanted to be. The light and swirling movement of the diamonds appeared to defy the laws of gravity, symbolizing their love of life. The commercial success of this line allowed Chopard to establish a respected position in the world of jewellery. Since then, the brand has continued to reinvent its models with shapes that are beautifully pure, joyful and light.

◀ Happy Clown pendant in yellow gold, with free-floating sapphire, emerald, ruby and diamonds.

Elephant pendant with three moving diamonds, diamond-set ear and sapphire eye.

Teddy-bear pendant in white gold with moving diamond.

Heart-shaped pendant in white gold with moving diamonds.

Chopard earrings ▶

B.ZERO

It is now over 20 years since Bvlgari launched its iconic B.zero ring, the luxury brand's best seller and probably the most recognizable piece in all its collections.

'B' AS IN BVLGARI

B.zero – what a strange name for a piece of jewellery! Where does it come from? The 'B' is for Bvlgari of course, followed by the zero, a nod to the new millennium that was just around the corner in 1999, the year of its launch.

THE COLOSSEUM AS SOURCE OF INSPIRATION

The B.zero consists of a spiral-shaped Tubogas cylindrical body held in place by two exterior bands. The Bvlgari name runs around the whole circumference of both outer bands and is engraved into the metal. The sinuous shape of the ring is inspired by the architecture of the Colosseum in Rome.

A SPECIAL TECHNIQUE

The body of the B.zero is produced using a technique known as Tubogas. Often used by Bvlgari, the name refers to a type of pipe used to transport gas in the early 20th century. The technique involves wrapping strips of metal around a cylinder. The edges of the strips interlock to create a visibly flexible exterior, while hiding the body of the central part.

The Bvlgari B.zero has been continually reinterpreted over the last two decades. Available in endless variations, the collection has given rise to more than a hundred different pieces of jewellery.

The Bvlgari B.zero has been continually reinterpreted over the last two decades.

2019: THE 20TH ANNIVERSARY

Bvlgari celebrated the 20th anniversary of the B.zero under the dome of the Auditorium Parco della Musica in Rome on 19 February 2019. To mark the occasion, it released a new solid-gold edition of the cult Tubogas flexible five-band ring, as a way of paying tribute to its first love. The ultimate finishing touch? The collector's mark 'XX Anniversary', delicately engraved on the inside of the last band, is visible only when the bands are jiggled between the fingers.

ICONIC ITERATIONS

Bvlgari B.zero in yellow gold and ceramic
One of the brand's most iconic models. Bvlgari introduced ceramics into the production of its iconic ring in 2010 to create a more avant-garde and sport-inspired look.

In the same year, to mark the tenth anniversary of the B.zero, Bvlgari collaborated with artist Anish Kapoor, who reinvented the icon in mirror-polished steel and rose gold.

Bulgari B.zero 'Save the Children' in silver and ceramic
In 2009, Bvlgari designed a more affordable B.zero 'Save the Children' ring, a philanthropic variation of the original piece. Profits from its sale were donated to the non-governmental organization of the same name that supports vulnerable children around the world.

B.zero worn as a pendant

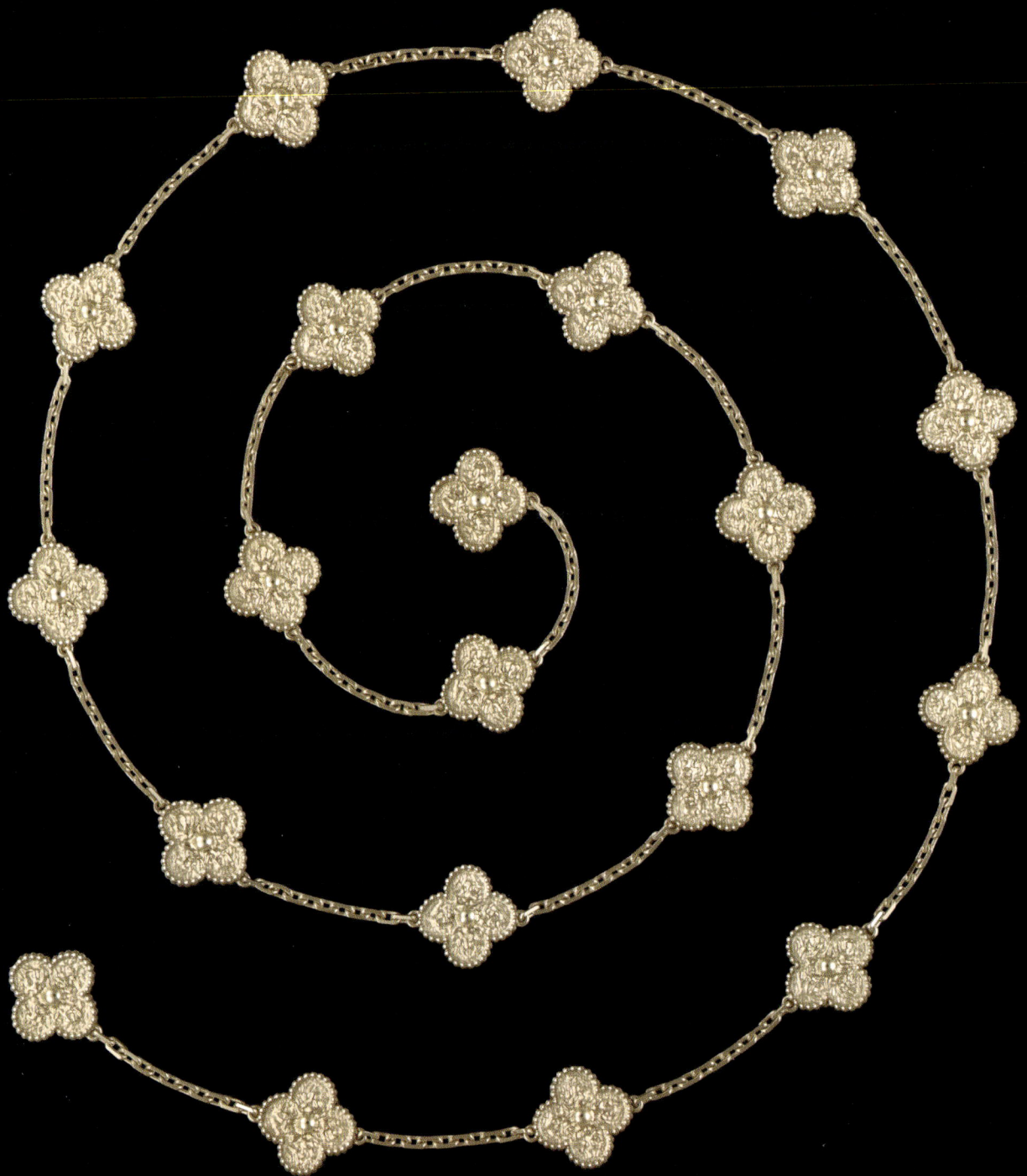

'To be lucky, you have to
believe in luck'
Jacques Arpels

THE ALHAMBRA COLLECTION

BY VAN CLEEF & ARPELS

A concept championed by the jewellery house, luck has often been a guiding light for Van Cleef & Arpels, inspiring some of its most iconic creations. Four-leaf-clover motifs first appeared in the jewellery house's designs as early as the 1920s and would later be followed by other symbols of good fortune such as talismanic wooden jewellery, charms and benevolent fairies. Jacques Arpels, the nephew of the founding couple and an avid collector, would often pick four-leaf clovers in his garden, offering them to his employees as good-luck charms.

LUCK – VAN CLEEF & ARPELS STYLE

In 1968, the jewellery house created its first Alhambra long necklace in yellow gold. Inspired by the four-leaf clover, it features 20 clover-shaped motifs in guilloched yellow gold, delicately edged with a border of gold beads. The necklace proved instantly popular and was worn by legendary personalities such as Princess Grace of Monaco and Françoise Hardy. The Van Cleef & Arpels design became known around the world as an iconic symbol of good luck. Catherine Cariou, the brand's heritage director, said in an interview that it was impossible to definitively identify the exact origins of the design, although two sources of inspiration are probable: the four-leaf clover, and the arabesque motifs in the gardens of the Alhambra, one of the most famous monuments of Islamic architecture located in Granada, Spain.

MOORISH ORIGINS

Alhambra ('red fortress' in Arabic) is the name of a majestic medieval citadel in Granada, Spain, and a jewel of Islamic architecture and art.

COLOURED CLOVER

Three years later, in 1971, colour was introduced into the Alhambra necklaces: the four-leaf clovers were decorated with hard gemstones such as malachite and lapis lazuli to add more sparkle to the outfits they were matched with.

VINTAGE ALHAMBRA

A major design change took place in 2001 when the classic Alhambra collection was reinterpreted to embrace the new millennium. The beaded trim of the quatrefoil motifs was replaced with a smooth, rounded finish to create a more modern look. This new line is known as Pure Alhambra, while the original designs were renamed Vintage Alhambra to distinguish the two collections.

A CONSTANTLY CHANGING LINE

The year 2002 saw the release of the Byzantine Alhambra collection, a more striking, geometric, discreet and simple version without the beaded outline or any interior decoration. With its openwork shape, this refined iteration showcases the outline of the clover shape.

And the jewellery house did not stop there. In 2006, for its centenary, the designs were further diversified with the Lucky Alhambra collection. The clover was joined by elements inspired by nature, such as butterflies, leaves and hearts, enhancing the jewellery with a multi-coloured palette and different shapes.

In the same year, Van Cleef decided to play with proportions through its Magic Alhambra collection, juxtaposing clover-shaped motifs of different sizes on the same piece.

ICONIC ITERATIONS

Today, more than half a century after it was first created, Alhambra jewellery continues to inspire multiple generations of men and women, who wear it both for its beauty and as a good-luck charm.

Necklace from the Magic Alhambra collection.

Long necklace from the Magic Alhambra collection with mother-of-pearl clover-shaped motifs.

Pure Alhambra pendant in white gold and mother-of-pearl

The smooth, rounded edges in this example are typical of the Pure Alhambra collection.

Force 10 bracelet in white gold and double-wrap
steel cable with ends in yellow gold.

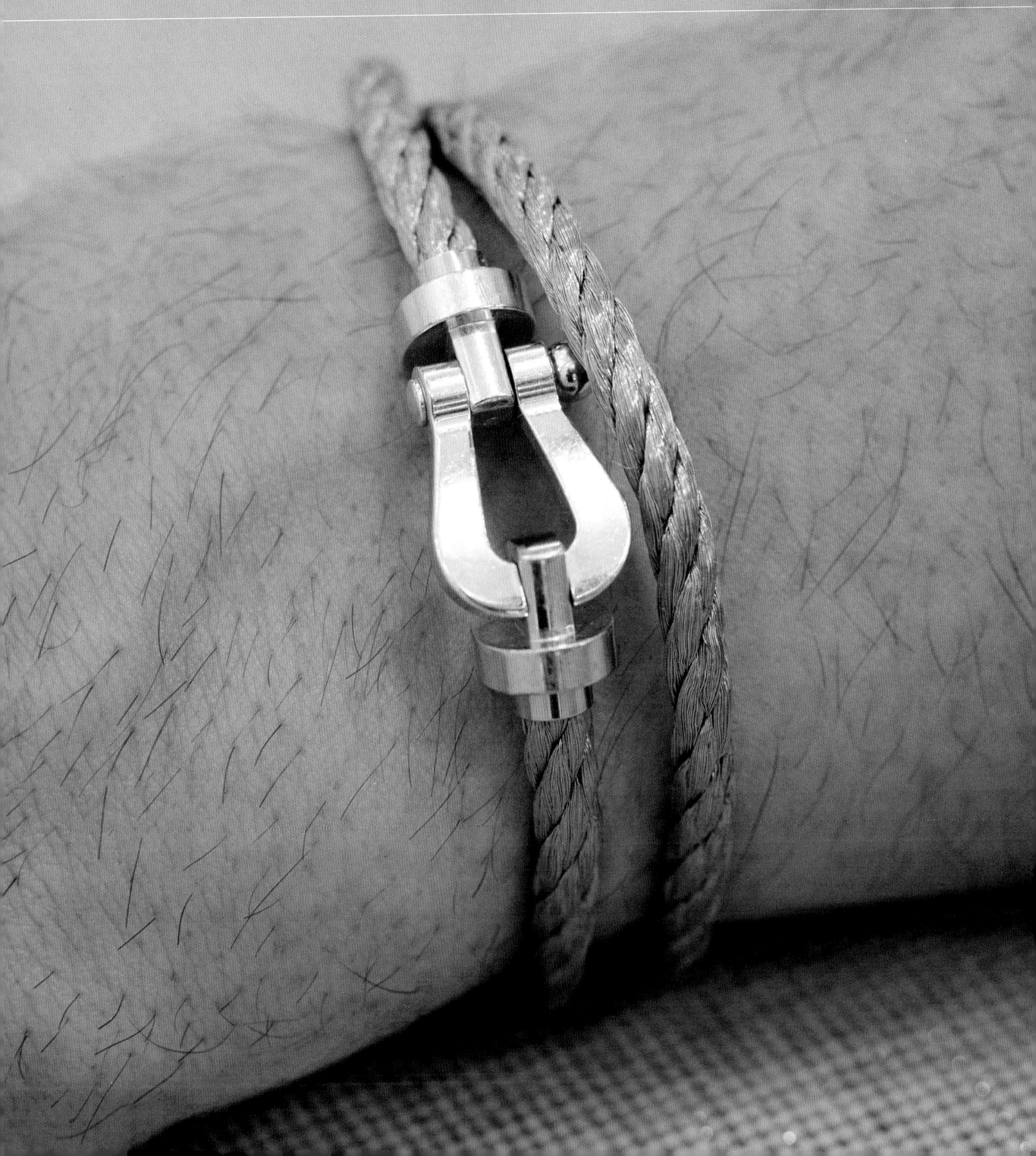

THE FORCE 10 BRACELET

The brand Fred, now part of luxury conglomerate LVMH, was founded in 1936 when Argentinian jeweller Fred Samuel opened his first shop at 6 rue Royale in the 8th arrondissement of Paris.

A BREATH OF FRESH AIR

It would be almost thirty years before the jewellery house developed its flagship piece: the Force 10 bracelet. Inspired by the sea, it featured a braided marine cable in steel, closed with a gold part resembling a boat shackle. At the time, it was a daring move to combine these two materials in the same piece of jewellery. The name 'Force 10' refers to the level on the Beaufort scale designating a storm with winds exceeding 48 knots (89km/h or 55mph). Samuel's love of sailing is clearly evident in the design of this piece.

THE ULTIMATE MIX-AND-MATCH MODEL

Casual and elegant, the model quickly became popular with both men and women, the key to its success being the interchangeability of the bracelet. The cord that attaches to the clasp can be easily removed by releasing the catch at either end of the closure and pulling it out. This versatility allows wearers to create infinite versions by combining the gold shackle with cables in different colours and finishes.

Today, the Force 10 is not just a bracelet, but a complete line ranging from everyday accessories (such as sunglasses) to *haute joaillerie* (high jewellery) pieces set with precious stones.

Fred signature, with production number.

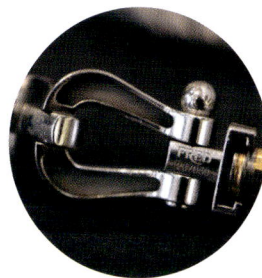

Interchangeable closure system.

Return to Tiffany collection, models from the 2000s.

Screwball keyring with oval tag.

RETURN TO TIFFANY

BY TIFFANY

Founded in 1837 by Charles Lewis, Tiffany & Co. is probably the most historically famous jewellery house in the United States thanks to its celebrated diamonds and engagement rings. The reputation of the luxury house peaked in 1961 with the excellent publicity it garnered from Audrey Hepburn. Dressed in Givenchy, she starred both outside and inside the store in the film Breakfast at Tiffany's, *an adaptation of the novel by Truman Capote. The LVMH group completed the acquisition of Tiffany & Co. in 2021.*

THE STORY OF A HEART

Diamonds are the specialty of the luxury house, but Tiffany became known to the general public through its silver jewellery. Several of its collections were reinterpreted in silver, the most iconic being Return to Tiffany, featuring the best-selling heart in the history of jewellery. The heart was inspired by a keyring created in 1966 and marketed as a Valentine present. It consisted of a heart tag in 14-carat gold attached to a chain. At the time, its price was only $11 (£4). A personalized number was engraved on the tag, alongside the words: 'Please return to Tiffany' so that the company could contact the owner and reunite them with their lost keys. In 1967, a version with an oval tag was released for men.

750 AND 925

In 1980, the keyring was redesigned into a necklace. The iconic Return to Tiffany heart was retained and still engraved with a number and the instructional wording, in combination with a longer chain.

In more recent collections, the serial number was replaced by the number '925' for pieces in silver, and '750' for pieces in gold.

From 1997, the Return to Tiffany collection diversified considerably with the inclusion of more than a hundred new pieces that are still iconic today, and it continues to be one of the best-selling lines of the jewellery house.

COSTUME JEWELLERY

BY CHANEL

Never one to shy away from a paradox, Gabrielle Chanel advocated simplicity and minimalism in her clothing but encouraged women to wear opulent jewellery that would not look out of place in a church treasury. Even today, the images of her wearing multiple strands of pearls still convey a certain authority and solemnity fitting for a high priestess of fashion. But there is much more to Chanel style than the long necklaces that Mademoiselle wore almost daily...

GRIPOIX

In 1924, Chanel met a family already known as one of the most important makers of refined jewels – Gripoix. At the time, it was famous for its particularly realistic imitation pearls, created by coating a glass 'core' with mother-of-pearl using a secret recipe. As these pearls were made in Paris, they became known as 'Perles de Paris'.

THE PEARL OF CLEOPATRA

Legend has it that Cleopatra hosted the most expensive banquet in history. She made a wager with Mark Antony to prove that Egypt still had considerable wealth. To demonstrate this, she invited him to attend a sumptuous meal worth more than 10 million sesterces. Mark Antony was sceptical but willingly accepted. He could only watch dumbfounded when the servants, instead of bringing Cleopatra exquisite dishes, offered her nothing more than a simple cup filled with vinegar. The queen then took one of the pearls hanging from her ear, dissolved it in the cup and drank it. She won the wager handsomely, as the pearls she wore were the largest known at the time and of inestimable value.

THE PEARLS OF GABRIELLE

And so, in the mid-1920s, Chanel became known for her faux pearls, regularly wearing imposing layered ropes of them. In her jewellery designs, she started to combine pearls with glass stones from the workshops of Maison Gripoix, which had developed a glass-working technique known as poured glass. This involved melting and enamelling glass in metal mountings, resulting in a finesse and fragility unheard of at the time.

INSPIRED BY HISTORY

Chanel closed its doors during the Second World War and would open them again only in 1953. The story of jewellery continued, however, thanks to one man, Robert Goossens, who worked for Mademoiselle until her death in 1971. The two lovers of history drew their inspiration from ancient forms of jewellery, including Etruscan, Egyptian and Merovingian. In 1956, Goossens bought a book on antique jewellery from a stall on the banks of the Seine. He then taught himself setting techniques from Asia inspired by the ancient Scythians, while his long necklaces and belts were directly drawn from the medieval period.

This resulted in the themes and motifs cherished by the couturière: the lion's head (related to Leo, her star sign), Byzantine crosses, and wire and enamelled *cloisonné* pieces. The manufacturing techniques used were borrowed from the world of *haute joaillerie*, and Chanel jewellery from this period is known for being as beautiful from the back as it is from the front.

'BIJOUX DE DIAMANTS'

In November 1932, Gabrielle Chanel held an exhibition entitled 'Bijoux de Diamants' (Diamond Jewels). It was held at the designer's home at 29 rue du Faubourg Saint-Honoré in Paris. These were her first *haute joaillerie* designs, made in partnership with Paul Iribe, her lover at the time. The professional body of the high jewellery industry (Chambre syndicale de la Haute Joaillerie) had not authorized the show, and she was ordered to dismantle the jewellery immediately afterwards and barred from selling it. It would be decades before the fashion house launched its own high jewellery line.

CHANEL LOGO

In 1983, Karl Lagerfeld was appointed creative director of Chanel. The designer's strength and success was derived from his ability to modernize the DNA of the fashion house without radically transforming it. He set about 'dissecting' the Chanel style: the chains, gold-tone metals, camellias, glass paste and pearls.

The early 1990s marked a turning point in the style of Chanel jewellery with, among other things, the arrival of Victoire de Castellane who had a strong influence on the designs of the luxury house. At the same time, a new fashion was emerging: the logo. Inspired by the trunk makers of the early 20th century who put their initials on luggage to differentiate it from other brands, couture houses now started to add their logos to clothes, bags and accessories. While Gabrielle Chanel had used her famous CC insignia for buttons and belts for many years, her initials and the name of the fashion house now started to appear everywhere. The message was clear: I buy Chanel and I want everyone to know it!

▲ Necklace with gold-tone metal pendant, decorated with crystals, poured glass and imitation pearls. This is similar to a model worn by Mademoiselle Chanel, made by Maison Gripoix, 1920s.

◄ Necklace designed by Robert Goossens. Inspired by the Byzantine cross, it is decorated with glass-paste cabochons, imitation emeralds, rubies and imitation white pearls, 1960s.

► Brooch in chased gold-tone metal, glass beads and cabochon, and imitation baroque pearls, made by Robert Goossens for Chanel in 1962. This model was worn by Romy Schneider on the cover of *Jours de France* magazine, 15 September 1962.

THE NEW WITH THE VINTAGE

In some collections from the early 1990s, glass paste was replaced with imposing resin cabochons. Miles of gold-tone metal chain were interwoven with leather, imitating the handles of the Classic Flap bag, to create belts, necklaces and even cufflinks. The long necklace worn by Mademoiselle was just as fresh as ever. She had loved it for its practicality, and Karl Lagerfeld paid homage to it by layering multiple versions in his runway shows and advertising campaigns. Two factors made these developments possible: the creative vitality of the designer, and the fashion for accessories. A new group of customers now had access to luxury fashion, and they wanted something fast: not just ready-to-wear but also accessories, objects that were much more affordable than haute couture. Right up until his last collection in 2019, Karl Lagerfeld never lost his love for accessories. And the enthusiasm for these items shows no sign of abating...

Set of haute couture jewellery made by Maison Gripoix for Chanel in the 1990s.

Iconic Camélia necklace in gold-tone metal and poured glass, made by Maison Gripoix for Chanel in the 1990s. The camellia was Chanel's favourite flower. She loved it for its simplicity and because it had neither scent nor thorns.

Drop earrings featuring the clasp of the Classic Flap bag in gold-tone metal set with crystals, suspending an imitation white pearl. Made by Maison Woloch for Chanel, Spring/Summer 1996 ready-to-wear collection.

Cuff bracelet in shaped composite, decorated with multi-coloured resin cabochons. Autumn/Winter 1990/91 ready-to-wear collection.

Rope-style cuff bracelet in gold-tone resin, decorated with glass-paste drops in shades of blue. Spring/Summer 1990 ready-to-wear collection.

Brooch in gilded bronze with turquoise-style glass beads, made by Robert Goossens. Spring/Summer 1959 collection.

► Chanel jewellery set from the 1980s in gold-tone metal, imitation gemstone glass-paste cabochons and imitation pearls. It is important to differentiate between cabochons made from glass paste and poured glass. Glass-paste cabochons are made in moulds and then added to the jewel, while poured glass is melted to fit within a wire outline of the jewel.

CHOMBERT
& ∫TERNBACH

Interview with fashion consultancy firm Chombert & Sternbach

Can you introduce yourself?

We are Dominique Chombert and Françoise Sternbach, experts in generalist fashion (leather goods, fur, couture, costume jewellery, accessories and so on).

Could you tell us about your roots?

I, Dominique, come from the world of fur; my father, Henri Chombert, was a renowned furrier who had some of the most famous people in the world as clients: Elizabeth Taylor and her husband, Ursula Andress, Johnny Hallyday and Sylvie Vartan, and Romy Schneider, to name a few. At the time, fur was not viewed with the distaste that it is today; our thinking about the animal world was different back then. Françoise comes from the world of retail and was a director of ready-to-wear stores. Her parents were antique dealers.

The two of us often visited the Drouot auction house and the Saint-Ouen flea market. As we travelled around these places, we realized that no one else was working in the specialty we had developed. At auctions, everything was sold in lots and the hammer prices were shamefully low. Following a chance meeting with an auctioneer, we embarked on our first sales in 1989. But we soon realized it was crazy to auction a sable coat in June, so Françoise suggested adding designer luggage to our sales. The auctioneer we were working with at the time asked us to hold a sale dedicated to accessories. This was so successful that we decided to set up our own fashion consultancy firm in 1993. At the time, everything was different; there were only two fashion consulting firms in existence but they operated in highly specialized fields that were slightly different from ours. We were keen to bring our vision to the industry as quickly as possible.

How did you get to where you are now?

As two women, it wasn't always easy for us to establish ourselves in the male-dominated auction world. But, most of all, it took a lot of hard work. When we were offered the first sale dedicated solely to costume jewellery, we had to find vast quantities of books and documentation to compensate for our lack of knowledge.

That's what makes this job interesting: doing something we love and constantly learning new things. The turning point for our firm definitely came with the launch of the first themed sales. At the time, we felt that there was a lot of enthusiasm for Louis Vuitton products. We then dedicated a sale exclusively to Hermès with around 300 lots: the result was mass hysteria, people fainting, emergency services, you name it. The sale was a massive success. This confirmed the vision we had set out with, and we then organized themed sales around other luxury brands: Chanel, Pierre Cardin and others. At the same time, we had the opportunity to conduct prestigious sales of pieces created by our favourite designer, Elsa Schiaparelli.

Have you noticed any changes in the market over the years?

It would be a lie to claim otherwise. In the 1990s, we were pretty much the only people doing this, and customers would travel from all over the world to attend our sales. International museums and collectors were on our client file. The real change came with the rise of resale sites on the internet. Human beings like to simplify their lives, and they now had the option of not having to travel, buying products remotely and getting them delivered to their home. This is a long way from how we view things as purists and collectors: acquiring an object involves contact with it, and the emotion it conveys. And as the storefronts of these platforms got bigger and bigger, sellers and buyers became less loyal: they could now sell and buy everywhere. What has really 'damaged' this market is the seller's ability to set whatever price they want: on certain platforms, astronomical prices are put on fairly classic models available in a multitude of copies. And even if these aren't sold, the customer and seller will use them as a yardstick. Fortunately, we have a circle of very loyal customers who prefer the purism of face-to-face sales.

Another problem we face is the issue of authenticity. Today, counterfeiting is rampant, and when we started it was much less prevalent. In most cases, people returned from a Mediterranean holiday with a crude and poor-quality counterfeit. But today, the level of deception is much more subtle. Counterfeit products are better and better made, creating standards of quality that are almost perfect compared to the authentic products.

'Counterfeit products are better and better made, creating standards of quality that are almost perfect compared to the authentic products.'

Is there an object that has made a particular impact on you in your career?

You can imagine that, after a career of more than thirty years in the field, I have held an unimaginable quantity of pieces in my hands. I won't focus on one piece in particular but on one sale instead: the one dedicated to Elsa Schiaparelli. We were lucky enough to exhibit the sale in the showroom of Azzedine Alaïa, who was a friend. We were surrounded by Schiaparelli's iconic designs. It was truly extraordinary. Apart from that, I would say the sale we held for the collection of the model Danielle Luquet de Saint Germain. She had an incredible archive of couture and ready-to-wear pieces from the greatest designers. Many of the models were sold straight to museums and private collections around the world.

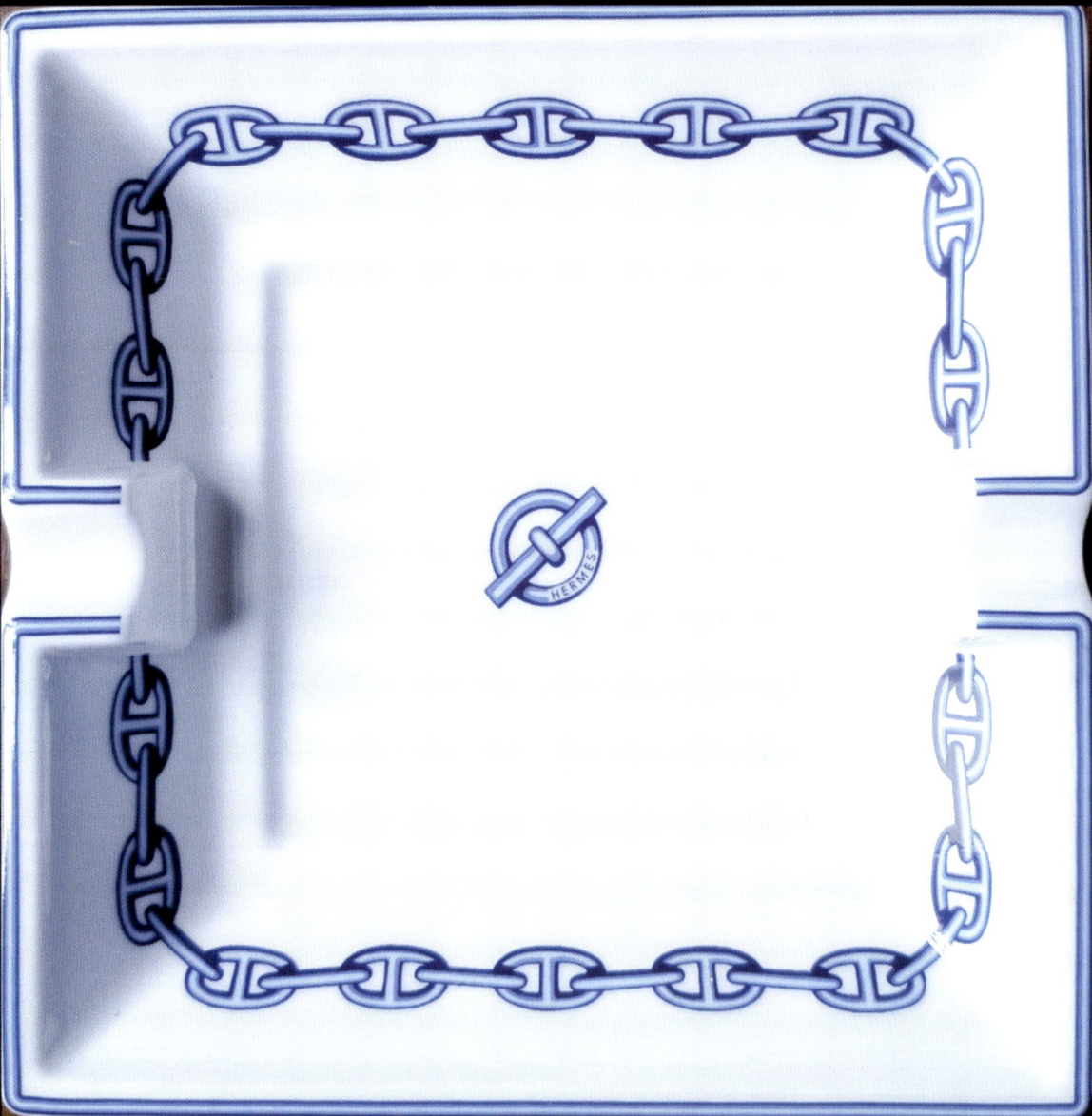

ASHTRAYS AND CHANGE TRAYS

BY HERMÈS

The first Hermès ashtrays were marketed in the early 1960s. The luxury house experimented with several sizes and shapes before the rectangle version, which is still made today, became the dominant model.

UNIQUE CREATIONS

The design is applied to the base of the ashtray with a chromolithography technique. These porcelain objects feature horses, hunting dogs, soldiers, yachts, flowers from every continent, Balinese dancers, jungle animals and underwater creatures, vintage cars and horse-drawn carriages, headwear from the Napoleonic era, and contemporary graphic designs. The image is framed with a hand-painted gold or silver trim.

The ashtray has a velvet goatskin base marked with one or more 'H'. The number of Hs indicate the complexity involved in making the object and determine its price. Some pieces are entirely hand painted and personalized. For example, the tiger in the 'Tigre royal' design has several very different expressions, sometimes happy, sometimes sad.

Hand-painted ashtray, with the 'Tigre royal' design.

DESIGNER PIECES

Hermès ashtrays feature a vast array of subjects. The first examples gave pride of place to the horse and carriage, not surprisingly, as the luxury house has always considered the horse to be its most demanding customer. Each unique image was then numbered.

Most of the designs were adapted from those created for silk scarves, while artists producing original designs were given enormous creative freedom. Some pieces were made especially for companies, which resulted in amusing juxtapositions of vastly different worlds. For example, the 'Fleury Michon' ashtray, named for a French charcuterie brand, depicted a farmer's wife feeding pigs.

FRENCH PORCELAIN

In 1770, kaolin deposits were discovered near the town of Limoges in France. The whiteness of the material allowed the production of a clay paste that was as light as the clay previously imported from China. French porcelain quickly became popular, especially at the court of Louis XV and Madame de Pompadour. In the 19th century, it was increasingly present in middle-class interiors and was seen as a sign of ostentatious wealth. When Hermès began to develop collections for the brand, it naturally turned to this premium material and called upon the best manufacturers in the field.

HONOURING TRADITION AND MODERNITY

One of the legends of the Hermès world was Philippe Ledoux. Born in 1903, to a wealthy French family living in Sheffield, England, he was taught to paint by his mother, an accomplished watercolourist, and at the École des Beaux-Arts in Paris. Hired in 1947 by Robert Dumas, then CEO of the brand, he designed more than ninety silk scarves, many of which were later adapted into ashtrays. His sources of inspiration were horses, boats and yachts. He died in 1975, and some of his designs were completed by his nephew Vladimir Rybaltchenko.

Other talented artists hired by Hermès include Joachim Metz, Julie Abadie, Henri d'Origny, Xavier de Poret and, more recently, Bali Barret and Agathe Gonnet. This is a non-exhaustive list, given that Hermès commissioned drawings from more than a hundred illustrators. Today, the Hermès ashtray collections include reissues of old pieces, often revisited in new colours, as well as highly contemporary designs, such as those of the English designer Jonathan Burton. Fun, fantastical and full of vibrant colour, his creations keep the feet of the venerable luxury house firmly in the present, while also projecting it into the future.

OLIBRIUS

Interview with Laurent Deutsch

How did you set up Olibrius?

In 2013, I was running a training company. Even though I loved my job, I was starting to get a bit bored. And then, by a twist of fate, an aborted trip to Berlin led me to visit the Saint-Ouen flea market, where I hadn't been for years. It was a revelation! At the end of my day there, something obvious had became clear: why not me?

Two months later, I opened Olibrius at the Vernaison market in Paris. The shop was originally filled with objects from my own personal collection. It was an immediate success. In 2016, I took a new step by opening a store in the Marais. The space was small but I had three beautiful shop windows where I had a lot of fun doing themed displays (animals, the gods of Olympus and so on). My clients loved it, and kids loved it. This wonderful adventure ended in 2022 when I decided to leave Paris. Olibrius continues to exist via an Instagram account and is permanently on show thanks to the visibility Raúl Barràgan offers me in his Opulence Luxury & Vintage store on rue Danielle Casanova in Paris.

What do you sell at Olibrius?

Tableware, decorative objects, smoking accessories, stationery and vintage pens from the brands Hermès, Christian Dior, Cartier, Gucci, Fendi and Asprey, but also objects by forgotten prestige brands such as Henry à la Pensée and Kirby, Beard & Co.

Which brands do you particularly like?

Rather than brands, I'm really just a lover of objects. Whether it's shapes, materials or styles, my tastes are very eclectic. I can find myself liking and combining minimalist pieces, if the work is of high quality, with baroque and over-the-top fantastical creations. That's why, out of all the brands I display and sell, my preference is for Christian Dior. The couturier's Maison, or homeware, line has always offered a really wide range of objects to its customers. I think I was one of the first resale dealers to take an interest in Christian Dior's lifestyle pieces. When I started my collection in the early 2000s, you could find Dior pieces for next to nothing, which is no longer the case today. My latest hobby-horse is pieces by Asprey London. There isn't much of it in France because the official supplier to the British Crown is rarely exported. My dream is to get their crystal decanter topped with a stag's head carved in solid silver.

What do your customers like?

You'd have to ask them!

Let's say that I hope to bring them a certain amount of expertise. I also try to offer them beautiful objects at reasonable prices. My real passion is buying, and if I want to buy a lot, items have to fly off the shelves!

OLIBRIUS
Opulence Luxury & Vintage
20 rue Danielle Casanova
75002 Paris
Instagram: @olibrius_decoration

Hermès placemats

Gucci animal stirrup cups

OBJECTS AND STYLES

BY CHRISTIAN DIOR

Christian Dior, the brilliant couturier of the New Look who restored Paris after the Second World War to its legendary glory, was also a shrewd businessman. Over the years, he created a complete world of refinement, combining not only haute couture and ready-to-wear, perfumes, jewellery and accessories, but also objects for the home and French-inspired lifestyle pieces.

THE DIOR WORLD

The Maison, or homeware, department was created in 1947 and located in a dedicated store known as Colifichets. Christian Dior was passionate about architecture and home decor: 'Living in a house that doesn't look like you is a bit like wearing someone else's clothes,' he once said. The idea of the store was that after trying on clothes or choosing outfits, customers could treat themselves to a little something or leave with gifts for friends and family.

From 1947 to the present day, tableware, household linen, smokers' items, luxury stationery and decorative objects have been developed under the leadership of Jean-Pierre Frère, Doris Brynner and then Cordelia de Castellane.

BOTH CLASSICAL AND REFINED

The Christian Dior Maison style is highly eclectic and suitable for both classic aristocratic interiors and more contemporary homes. A wide range of materials are used: silver and silver-plated metal for brass and copper pieces, porcelain, earthenware and crystal for tableware, and Plexiglas and dried flowers for beautiful trays that celebrate nature.

COLLECTIONS THAT TELL THE DIOR STORY

The Maison collections showcase Christian Dior's tastes and are another way of telling his life story. There are many objects displaying flowers, including roses and lily of the valley, which reminded Monsieur Dior of his childhood and the garden at his home in Granville, Normandy.

Montelupo earthenware:
a tribute to Italian majolica.

Plate from the Milly-la-Forêt dinner
service, celebrating Monsieur
Dior's passion for flowers, including
lily of the valley.

Pieces from the
Grand Salon dinner
service.

THE GRAND SALON DINNER SERVICE

Certain collections were sometimes specially created for an important event. The
Grand Salon dinner service, one of the brand's most beautiful, was originally designed
for a gala dinner organized by the American Embassy at the Château de Versailles on
3 November 1993. Baptised 'Versailles and Royal Tables in Europe', the aim of the dinner
was to showcase the excellence of European tableware. Each piece was hand painted
with 24-carat gold.

Following the dinner, and noting the success of the Grand Salon service, the House
of Dior decided to offer it to the public in a more affordable version, with the pattern
reproduced using the chromolithography technique.

ITALIAN EARTHENWARE

From the early days of the Maison department, Dior used prestigious Italian ceramic
companies that created exclusive models for the brand. These entirely hand-painted
designs were always brush-signed 'Christian Dior', and often referenced Italian splen-
dours of the past. The magnificent models made by the Montelupo factory pay homage
to the age-old tradition of majolica.

Ceramic techniques also allow for great creativity, which can be seen in the superb
dinner services imitating malachite and lapis lazuli.

THE MONOGRAM
The decorative
monogram featuring
the interlocking letters
D.I.O.R. is omnipresent
in the Dior Maison
collections. It was
inspired by a famous
brooch created by
Christian Dior in 1951.

Plexiglas tray with dried
plants, designed by
Doris Brynner
for Dior.

The iconic Dior Maison monogram is displayed not only on plates but also on all types of objects, from ashtrays to decanters.

THE 'CANNAGE' COLLECTIONS

Dior took his inspiration from Second Empire furniture, which often featured the clever weaving of rattan and cane. This woven motif was generously used in the decoration of the store on avenue Montaigne, not only in the furniture, but also in the filigree patterns on wallpaper friezes.

The cannage motif was quickly introduced into the luxury house's objects for the home. In the 1970s, it commissioned the famous designer Gabriella Crespi to design a modernized cannage collection: she inserted the famous weaving between two Plexiglas sheets to create a collection of trays, desk accessories and umbrella stands. Later, the pattern was also woven through objects in crystal.

The cannage motif even became a star signature of Dior leather goods, celebrated for example in the Lady bag created in homage to Princess Diana.

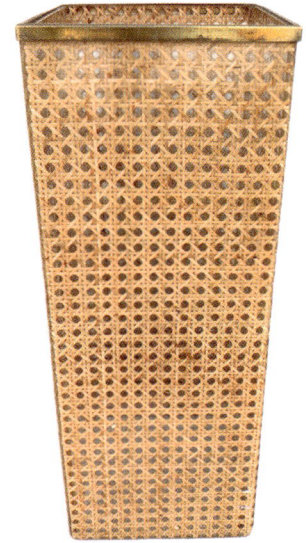

Umbrella stand designed by Gabriella Crespi.

Metal Christian Dior plate with logo.

Change tray in silver-plated metal.

Limoges porcelain bowl, with logo in yellow gold.

SILVER AND SILVER-PLATED METAL

Silver and silver-plated pieces (the latter being more common) were predominant in the Dior Maison collections until the early 2000s. They borrowed from both Western metalworking traditions as well as those of North Africa and Asia (the hammered metalwork found in the Maghreb and India was a source of inspiration).

Many different designers have created beautiful silver-plated metal objects for Dior – for example Maria Pergay's famous jewellery box decorated with two Roman coins joined by a chain.

Today, metal objects are less common in the offerings of Dior, but it is likely that the most beautiful examples will be reissued sooner or later as the luxury house is keen to keep its immense heritage alive and preserve it for posterity.

HIGHLY COVETED PIECES

Today, Dior Maison pieces are collected by many connoisseurs around the world. A first auction dedicated solely to this theme was organized by an auction house in October 2015.

Dior duck in painted porcelain. ▶

> *'Whoever wishes to foresee the future must consult the past; for human events ever resemble those of preceding times.'* Machiavelli

JEAN-SÉBASTIEN MOISY

Azzedine Alaïa shared the vision of poet and political thinker Niccolò Machiavelli, and it was through talking to the famous couturier that I realized to what extent the past has played a role in today's designs, without knowing at the time that it was going to become my mantra.

Fashion and history are inextricably linked.

For more than ten years, I have been lucky enough to earn my living from these two passions. Like an archaeologist, I tell the story of the object that I have in my hands. For example, this can involve explaining the background to the Saint Laurent safari jacket that a customer wore on nights out at the iconic Castel club, or telling the story of the Kelly bag that a customer inherited from her grandmother. I believe that these pieces, which have witnessed life events, but also great moments in history, are worthy of museum status. What would Grace Kelly's pregnancy have been without her famous handbag, or early 20th-century transport without the Louis Vuitton travel bag? As a fashion expert, I know that in this area there is no absolute truth. After completing a master's in art history, I joined the fashion consultancy firm of Dominique Chombert & Françoise Sternbach.

Thirteen years later, I am fortunate to be still doing this job with the same passion as in the early days, always on the lookout for exceptional pieces.

2015 was a turning point in my professional career: I had the opportunity to hold the world's first auction dedicated solely to Chanel costume jewellery and, in the same year, I became the youngest expert in my field in France.

At the age of just 24, I must admit that it was difficult to be taken seriously at first, as the expert appraisal profession in the collective imagination is always connected with a 'wise' person and therefore...someone generally older!

However, I know that passion can overcome the issue of age, and that it is often more formative and motivating than years of experience: I can still see myself spending whole nights devouring archive after archive, proving that curiosity is the most powerful driver of knowledge.

Today, pure authenticity lies at the heart of my profession, as we face the new phenomenon of 'superfakes'. These near-perfect imitations are seriously undermining the resale market. The many different players in this market also make it more difficult to understand.

I organize training courses and lectures around the world, and my passion for these events burns as brightly as ever. I hope that here I have succeeded in conveying to you the love I have for my profession, and for the pieces that say so much about the era that created them.

Jean-Sébastien Moisy (left)
and Raúl Barràgan Sanz

ACKNOWLEDGEMENTS

First of all, I would like to thank my family who have helped me travel the world, from exhibition to exhibition, and who have allowed me to develop professionally without ever believing that anything was impossible. And especially my grandmother 'Nany' who taught me the love of a well-made seam, and whose advice I will never forget: 'When you buy a piece [of fashion or art], it should embody the soul of the fashion house or artist, otherwise it's of no interest.' She has been my guide.

I would also like to thank Dominique Chombert and Françoise Sternbach who both, in their different ways, have helped me to achieve my professional potential. Françoise for the long hours spent at her desk, as she turned garments inside out to explain the basics to me. And Dominique for having introduced me to the workings of a fashion consultancy firm but, above all, for her almost blind faith in me.

Thank you to Raúl who believed in me years ago, long before I did. A simple professional meeting on social media can sometimes lead to an exceptional friendship. Eight years later, we ended up working together, and during this process, I have once again witnessed your unwavering support. You transform my doubts and fears into certainties and confidence.

Thank you to my partner, Jean-Luc, who never complained about the evenings I spent reading with the lights on late into the night in our studio apartment. And who valiantly puffed and panted under the weight of those same books each time we moved house. But who, above all, has been there to support me every step of the way.

Finally, thank you to Isabelle, who shared her knowledge from the very first time we met and whose love of excellence she applies to everything she does, as do I.

INSTAGRAM
@louisdoisemont

Jean-Sébastien Moisy

RAÚL BARRÀGAN SANZ

My name is Raúl and I am the founder of Opulence Luxury & Vintage. A store owner and entrepreneur of Spanish origin, I arrived in Paris in 2009 after a career in marketing consumer goods. In 2016, I decided to start a new adventure, guided by my passion for luxury and rare vintage pieces. After months of searching, I found the right premises for my first store on rue Réaumur, in the heart of the 2nd arrondissement in Paris, and introduced the public to the collection of vintage bags and accessories I had built over the years.

Opulence Luxury & Vintage is the ideal destination for French and international customers looking for vintage and pre-loved pieces appraised by experts. We guarantee the authenticity of all our items, which gives our customers complete confidence. Following the rapid success of the first boutique and building on the reputation I had gained at trade fairs in London, Monaco and Paris, I was able to open two more stores over the next few years, one on the Île Saint-Louis, and a third, larger one on rue Danielle Casanova, a stone's throw from the legendary place Vendôme. In this last store, the focus is more on ready-to-wear.

Experience has shown me the interest lovers of fashion have in the history of each piece, from its design to its production, from its cult appearance to the style ambassadors who wore it. And so the desire emerged to create a book on vintage luxury goods that would allow me to reveal the fascinating secrets behind iconic pieces.

It is impossible to cover everything in a single book, so for this first opus we have selected pieces that you have probably already seen on the street, in a magazine, in the wardrobe of a loved one, or even in your own!

Raúl Barràgan Sanz, in front of one of his stores in Paris.

ACKNOWLEDGEMENTS

No project happens in isolation...And it is for this reason that I have so many people to thank: those women and men who have supported me throughout the journey that led to the creation of Opulence Luxury & Vintage and the publication of this book.

First of all, I would like to thank my parents and my family for their unconditional support. You gave me the resources to achieve my dreams. You are always there when I need you, discreet but strong and caring. You have given me the security and confidence to have the strength to keep moving forward.

To Paloma, my mother. You who, without hesitation, will jump on a plane to be by my side at a trade show, a fair or an event. You who, without complaining, will help me set up stands, create window displays, clean handbags and carry suitcases full of treasures during our trips to London, Monaco or Milan, and always with a smile!

To you, my consignors, for the enormous trust you place in me, because I know that it is not always easy to hand over your Birkin bag to a complete stranger.

To you, my customers. Without you I wouldn't be here. Thank you for your enthusiasm, your questions, your encouragement and your messages. If only you knew how happy I am to see you leave one of my stores, satisfied with your finds.

To you, my colleagues. Thank you for being there – conscientious, concerned, involved, welcoming and competent.

To Laurent. You always have good advice to give. All year long, you put up with my worries and crazy ideas with perspective and good humour. Thank you also for reading and rereading the pages of this book.

To Jean-Sébastien, my friend and co-author of this book. It all started eight years ago with an Instagram post! And today you have become one of the most important people in my life. You have never held back from sharing your immense knowledge with me, and you have always supported and helped me, even before our friendship took off. I loved creating this book with you.

And finally, thank you, Xavier, my partner. You are far removed from the world of fashion, but your curiosity and concern have pushed you to want to read and reread the pages of this book. You have a knack for helping me to solve problems. You are always there to help me move forward and grow.

I have a wonderful support network of loving people around me. And I am so happy to wake up each morning and get to love my job. I hope that through this book I have been able to transmit some of my enthusiasm, just as I try to do each day at Opulence Luxury & Vintage.

Raúl Barràgan Sanz

Picture credits

Measurement conversions

Metric	Imperial
10cm	3.9in
20cm	7.9in
30cm	11.8in
40cm	15.7in
50cm	19.7in
60cm	23.6in
70cm	27.6in
80cm	31.5in
90cm	35.4in
1m	3.3ft

Metric	Imperial
1km	0.6 miles
50km	31.1 miles
100km	62.1 miles
500km	310.7 miles
1kg	2.2lb
5kg	11lb
10kg	22lb
20kg	44.1lb
30kg	66.1lb
40kg	88.2lb

Originally published by Editions Larousse in 2024

First published in Great Britain in 2025 by Mitchell Beazley, an imprint of
Octopus Publishing Group Ltd
Carmelite House
50 Victoria Embankment
London EC4Y 0DZ
www.octopusbooks.co.uk

An Hachette UK Company
www.hachette.co.uk

The authorized representative in the EEA is Hachette Ireland, 8 Castlecourt Centre, Dublin 15, D15 XTP3, Ireland (email: info@hbgi.ie)

Copyright © Larousse 2024

Distributed in the US by Hachette Book Group
1290 Avenue of the Americas, 4th and 5th Floors
New York, NY 10104

Distributed in Canada by Canadian Manda Group
664 Annette St., Toronto, Ontario, Canada M6S 2C8

ISBN 978 1 84091 965 3
eISBN 978 1 84091 966 0

A CIP catalogue record for this book is available from the British Library.

Printed in China
10 9 8 7 6 5 4 3 2 1

For Larousse
Publishing Director: Carine Girac-Marinier
Editor: Maëva Journo
Graphic design and layout: Florence Le Maux
Production: Rebecca Dubois

For Mitchell Beazley
Publishing Director: Alison Starling
Project Editor: Sarah Reece
Assistant Editor: Ellen Sleath
Translation from French: Alison Murray in association with
    First Edition Translations Ltd
Creative Director: Jonathan Christie
Designer: Jeremy Tilston
Senior Production Manager: Katherine Hockley